BEING A DISTANCE SON OR DAUGHTER

A Book for ALL Generations

Helen Ellis M.A.

First published in New Zealand by Distance Families Publishing

ISBN
978-0-4736234-0-1 Paperback
978-0-4736234-1-8 Paperback - Print on demand
978-0-4736234-2-5 E-book Epub

Cover and illustrations designed by Cath Brew at drawntoastory.com
Cover photograph: Shutterstock

Disclaimer
Some of the quotations from contributors have been edited for reasons of clarity. Names of some contributors have been changed for reasons of privacy.

PRAISE FOR

Being a Distance Son or Daughter - a Book for ALL Generations

"What an amazing reference document for distance sons and daughters! It covers all aspects of life (literally from life to death!), common issues facing expats (such as multicultural families), and things which happen in all families (crises and relationship breakdowns) but take on added complexity with geographical separation. It will sit on my bookshelf ready to be consulted when I need a solution or a perspective that takes into account the particular situation of a distance family."

Bridget Romanes
Principal, Mobile NZ
www.mobile-relocation.com

"I'm so glad that Helen wrote this book. Being away from parents is a challenge that accompanies so many in their expat experience (myself included!). Helen walks us through this journey with empathy, insights and reflections from researchers and her own valuable experience. I'll recommend it to my clients and I will consult it very often."

Gabriela Encina
Psychologist/Online Counseling for Women Abroad
www.gabriela-encina.com

"How I wish I'd had this book when I started living around the world as a Distance Daughter! Ellis offers rich reflection, useful resources, strategies for stronger communication, and paths to deeper connection with those we love. Essential for anyone considering a move overseas, or for any parent with expat children."

Margaret Davis Ghielmetti
Author of *Brave(ish): A Memoir of a Recovering Perfectionist*
www.margaretghielmetti.com

"Helen Ellis's book *Being a Distance Son or Daughter* - a Book for ALL Generations leaves no stone unturned. This is a deeply comprehensive look at the challenges of being a distance son or daughter, including straight talk on anything from finance, in-laws, holiday visits to death. The gift in this book is that being armed with these informed perspectives allows us all to make the most of our relationships, no matter where we are."

Sundae Schneider-Bean, LLC
Intercultural Strategist and Podcaster
www.sundaebean.com

"I have been a global citizen for much longer than I was a stationary citizen. Not fully belonging anywhere is a feeling I am comfortable with, and even crave if I stay too long in any one place. My husband and children understand this feeling, even if they experience it somewhat differently. My family and oldest friends love telling stories about my newest location but really know very little about my experiences. It has always been this way. Until I read Helen's book, I was unaware that the way I felt and bumbled through my oldest relationships was common to serial expats. This book provided insight into how others have found solutions to navigate distant relationships in a way that can be mutually satisfying. As my own adult children start to scatter around the globe, I have the advantage of being able to experience their joy secondhand, combined with new knowledge on managing our future distant relationships. What an excellent life resource!"

Ana McGinley
Author of *Parental Guidance: Long Distance Care for Aging Parents*
www.parentalguidance.info

"With *Being a Distance Son or Daughter* Helen manages to bring to life not only the different generations and points of view but also the reflections and learning that can come out of these complex relationships. This book is a wonderful addition to the mobile community and Helen shares with us intimate stories to bring light and give us tips on how to keep up with the changes in each life involved in this big family living apart - but together."

Carolina Porto
International Transition Mentor
Author of *Lar Mundo Afora* and *Un Hogar Lejos De Casa*
www.carolinaporto.net

"An incredibly rich and comprehensive resource for Distance Families! Ellis covers detailed aspects of expat family life and unpacks complicated emotions along this journey with empathy, depth, and reflection. This book often moved me to tears; some scenarios, especially those of navigating visits back home, were all too familiar as a distance daughter for over 20 years. This book belongs on the bookshelf of every expat who moves abroad!"

Mariam Navaid Ottimofiore
Author of *This Messy Mobile Life*

"Being a Distance Daughter and sibling now for over 23 years, I thought I had a pretty good understanding and enough experience on how to navigate my relationships. Helen's book gave me new perspectives, different levels of understanding and an insight into topics and situations that I may or may not encounter in the future. Helen does not shy away from saying it as it is; the reality and raw truth of how one may be thinking or feeling, but not necessarily openly acknowledging, left me pondering on the past, present and future of my distance relationship with my parents and siblings. Thank you, Helen, for writing such an honest, thought provoking and supportive book. A must-read and one I will refer to often. I wish this had been written years ago!"

Navine Eldesouki
Founder of Coffee with an Expat
www.coffeewithanexpat.com

To my family... near and far.

CONTENTS

FOREWORD

One of my greatest intellectual joys is when I come across something that sparks a "Wow! That's eye opening and thought provoking" response. I had that reaction with *Being a Distance Grandparent*, Helen Ellis's first book in her series about family members living abroad. Much to my delight, I experienced it again while reading the manuscript for this book, *Being a Distance Son or Daughter*.

The subtitle for both these books is *A Book for ALL Generations*, as it will be again for the forthcoming third book in the series, *Being a Distance Grandchild*. For that matter, although Helen focuses on an understanding of the relationships between out-of-country family members in unique and significant ways, I envision the series subtitle could be *A Book for ANYONE Interested in Relationships*.

Photo courtesy of Charl Durand (www.charldurand.com)

As someone who has studied and written about relationships for many decades myself, I know that Helen's academic background, research, personal experiences, insights, and a compilation of others' anecdotes come together in powerful ways to help anyone be better at 'moving around' a relationship.

Here is what I mean about moving around a relationship. If you are standing in front of a statue, for example, Rodin's 'The Thinker', and I am standing behind it, our respective views in describing what we see will be quite different: one is seeing a pensive pose; the other is seeing buttocks and a spine. It is not until both of us have viewed the statue from shared angles and perspectives that we can begin to have a full appreciation of how each of us is experiencing what viewing the statue means. In other words, have empathy for the other's viewpoint.

The importance of having empathy in relationships cannot be overstated. As Helen writes, "The mantra of my Distance Family book series is:

With knowledge comes understanding
With understanding comes empathy
And empathy is a good thing for Distance Families."

In this book, *Being a Distance Son or Daughter*, Helen helps the reader to appreciate and develop empathy and to learn a host of skills. In addition, she provides a practical toolkit with strategies and hands-on techniques to understand and strengthen, not only distance familial relationships, but *all* important relationships. Like I said, Wow!

Karen L. Rancourt, Ph.D.
Advice Columnist, "Ask Dr. Gramma Karen",
hosted by *GRAND* Magazine
Author of *It's All About Relationships: New Ways to Make Them Healthy and Fulfilling, at Home and at Work*
https://karenrancourt.com

ABOUT THIS BOOK

"Even as migrants close the distance between self and other in the host country, they open up a distance between themselves and where they once lived. For them, negotiating these different forms of distance is an ongoing challenge."
Diane Comer, *The Braided River*

This is a book about the sons and daughters who leave home to live temporarily or permanently in an expat/migrant setting - the *Distance Sons and Daughters* who are geographically separated from their extended families (*Distance Families*).

For some Distance Sons and Daughters, talking about the family back home is like opening a proverbial can of worms. For others, it's a deep and wrenching heartache that never goes away. And while some Distance Families are accepting of the geographical separation and everyone does what they can to make things work, it's not a given. In this book I explore the 'how it is' and offer some 'how to' advice.

For Distance Sons and Daughters: this book acknowledges and empathises with the dilemmas of expat/migrant life and being a Distance Son or Daughter. It also aims to inject a sense of sureness about how to navigate your family role. Sureness delivers freedom from doubt, a belief in yourself and an assurance that you're doing your best - which is all that can be expected.

For Distance Families (grandparents, parents, siblings and extended family): I hope this book will deliver a deeper insight into the world of your Distance Family - in a way that family members may hesitate to share with you directly.

Empathy - the Goal

"Empathy pertains to the vicarious experiences of thoughts, feelings, emotions and attitudes; understanding by putting oneself in another's position... To empathize means I momentarily suspend my 'me-ness', and I totally focus on the other person."
Dr Karen L. Rancourt, professor of psychology

In line with Dr Rancourt's definition of empathy, the mantra of my Distance Family book series is:

With knowledge comes understanding
With understanding comes empathy
And empathy is a good thing for Distance Families

Terminology

"Our moving vocabulary is made up of different terms - to immigrate, to migrate, to flee, to rotate, to expatriate, to seek refuge or the chance to build a better future. As a result, multi-mobile families sometimes feel that because they all move under different circumstances with varying motives and rationales, it is hard to understand the commonalities that they share as a result of all their moves."
Mariam Navaid Ottimofiore, *This Messy Mobile Life*

Mariam is right.

In this book I interweave the terms 'expat' and 'migrant', focusing on neither one nor the other. Mawuna Koutonin is an online editor commenting on African racial issues. In a confronting article in *The Guardian*, he claims that the term 'expat' is reserved exclusively for white-skinned people and that 'immigrants' are everyone else. Koutonin's comments - and others who are creating awareness of the topic under the hashtag #expatxmigrant - provide evidence of the good and bad of globalisation and how it can be perceived. I acknowledge their sentiments. My own view of these terms is purely practical.

In broad terms, this book defines expats and migrants in the following way:

- Expats are those who are 'on the move' and don't foresee their current location as their forever landing place.
- Migrants are people who see where they live now as more than likely their long-term landing place.

I speak for them all.

Who *Isn't* Featured in This Book

It is important to address this. Distance Familying is a broad topic and I haven't attempted to write about *all* global Distance Sons and Daughters. With a few exceptions, Distance Sons and Daughters with the following backgrounds do *not* feature:

- Those from Asian countries with a strong culture of filial piety (respect and care of elders)
- Those left behind because of war, terrorism or climate change
- Those from developing, remittance-receiving (money sent home by migrants) nations

Distance Familying is rarely a walk in the park - for any of us. However, circumstances of war, terrorism, racism and culturally and economically affected communities cannot be compared with the lives of the mainly Western Distance Sons and Daughters featured in this book.

The unwilling

There is another category left out: Distance Sons and Daughters who resist working on family relationships. Writer Jessica Wildfire opened her article 'You Don't Have to Love Your Family' with: "Our culture has brainwashed us all to worship at the altar of family kinship. Why? No innate reason exists for loving your family, or even liking them, except genetics. And that's a shitty reason."

The Distance Sons and Daughters who align themselves with Jessica's article are also *not* the subjects of this book and, in fairness, aren't likely to read it either. Everyone is entitled to their opinion. Their familial bridges have sadly been disassembled, for whatever reason. We all have choices, and for some, intentional estrangement, or a version of it, is their preferred stance.

I devote this book to intergenerational Distance Families whose journeys may not be in meticulous alignment, but like the wobbly wheels of a well-loved, battered old tricycle, are at least heading in a forward direction.

Reading Recommendations

I hope my book series will be super helpful, but I encourage you to not stop there. Along the way I'll recommend a handful of invaluable books - I'm a fan of learning from experts. As the old saying goes, there's power in knowledge. All titles are recapped in the *Resources* at the end of the book.

A Story Behind the Book's Title

I could have titled this book *Being a Distance Child* and it would have been technically correct. But that comes with a 'young' veneer, and in reality the subjects of this book are in their 30s, 40s and 50s.

Instead, I chose 'son' and 'daughter' because this is a book about relationships. That includes Distance Daughters-in-law, Sons-in-law and partners too. They all have a place in this book; they are vital actors in the Distance Family story. 'Son' and 'daughter' are shown in that order for no other reason than the words flow more easily.

I acknowledge that the book's title isn't gender expansive. I do not wish to offend or exclude anyone and later I will share the backstory of an alternative title I considered: *Being a Distance Child (of).*

My Story

I am a cheerleader for ALL generations of Distance Families. I understand how it is for them and I want to help all generations to accept their roles, flourish and thrive.

Me the Distance Parent and Grandparent

When my husband, Clive, and I married in 1989, it was second time around for both of us. We each brought to our union a son and daughter. Clive is older than me and in the year of our wedding our children turned 21, 20, 5 and 3 years. We had no children together.

One or other of our children has lived for months, years or permanently in England, Scotland, Northern Ireland, Sweden, U.S.A., Thailand, Democratic Republic of Congo, Senegal, South Sudan or Pakistan.

These days they're in their 50s and 30s, and three of our four adult children and five of our six grandchildren (ranging from 5 to 22 years old) live in the U.S.A., Scotland and England. The last time we had our four adult children together for a meal was in 2009. We've never had a full family reunion.

To our four overseas grandchildren, Clive and I are these unfamiliar then familiar again faces with strange accents who touch down for a week or three and then disappear again. Over the years we've made 18 visits.

Closer to home, I have also been a fully-fledged, card-carrying 'in-country' grandmother for our two New Zealand-raised granddaughters (22 and 20 years old) - albeit a stepgrandmother. In the early days I did all the typical things grandmothers do, but because of our odd family dynamics, it happened in tandem with raising two teenagers. One of these granddaughters, who was born in Scotland, has lately floated between the country of her birth and her 'home'.

Me the researcher and anthropologist

"Anthropology is an intellectual framework that enables you to see around corners, spot what is hidden in plain sight, gain empathy for others, and fresh insight on problems... These ideas are as useful in making sense of an Amazon warehouse as in an Amazon jungle."
Gillian Tett, anthropologist

I am an anthropologist, or more accurately, a fledgling anthropologist. As a mature student I tackled a BA followed by a master's, both majoring in social anthropology.

Anthropology comes with a burst of exotic mystery, conjuring up images of safari jacket-clad, camera-carrying, patriarchal white male academics living with the 'natives' in far-off jungles. Once this was true.

Commentators explain anthropology as "making the strange familiar". Individuals with an anthropological bent ask a lot more 'whys' than most and have a desire to understand situations, cultures and ways of living from every angle. A university colleague, sensory anthropologist Dr Ruth Gibbons, writes of anthropologists who "live in the between". That is me. I am not the topic or the subject of this book; I live *in* the topic. I am neither a fully-fledged 'insider' nor a fully-fledged 'outsider'. Or to borrow a phrase from Norwegian anthropologist Thomas Hylland Eriksen, I have a desire to understand connections "within and *between*" societies. My society of choice is Distance Families.

Me the Distance Daughter

For 18 months in the late 70s/early 80s, I was a Distance Daughter. I went on my OE (Overseas Experience) after I was first married, a rite of passage working holiday in those days for 'down under' New Zealanders, Australians and South Africans. It was the norm to arrive without a job, spend a couple of nights in a hostel and figure things out from there. We had a string of temporary jobs, working for most of the year and holidaying in the summer.

We would record newsy updates onto cassette tapes and send them back home, but if the batteries were running low, we'd end up posting something that sounded like a slow-motion movie soundtrack. No fun for the folks back home who were eagerly waiting for any morsel of news.

Despite our very basic living conditions and temporary jobs, I relished the freedom and adventure. But with another winter around the corner, home beckoned, and I returned to New Zealand. I've lived there ever since.

COVID-19: the Great Disrupter

The COVID-19 pandemic affected every geographically scattered family, including my own. Do you remember those whirligig playground fixtures that have all but disappeared from neighbourhood landscapes? Being a member of a Distance Family during COVID-19 was like being forced to ride on a whirligig, with no freedom to hop on or off.

In my case, I became a Distance Daughter again when my widowed mother, who lives just 20 minutes away, turned into a 'distance' parent for months on end thanks to lockdown rules. And so began the daily FaceTime calls.

So little has been written about Distance Families that before I make predictions about the future, it's necessary to address what is, what has been and what we've all known. Whatever is new or altered in the future is judged by and compared to what *was*.

I will revisit the pandemic at the close of this book.

Reflection

Each book in the Distance Family series finds me wearing different hats. Most of the time I'm the author telling *your* generation's story, and I include research and commentary from scholars, experts and those who've walked your journey. In this book, it's all about 'how it is' for Distance Sons and Daughters. Occasionally, though, remembering the mantra of my book series, I'll don my distance parent/grandparent hat and share another perspective.

Let's dig in.

1. UNDERSTANDING DISTANCE PARENTS AND DISTANCE GRANDPARENTS

"If we assume too readily that we can see things from others' points of view we end up seeing them from merely a variation of our own. We are often told we should put ourselves in the shoes of others but stepping into someone's footwear is not the same as getting inside their mind. We have to get beyond imagining how things would look to us from an unfamiliar viewpoint and really try to understand how they look to others for whom the landscape is home."
Dr Julian Baggini, *How the World Thinks: A Global History of Philosophy*

In *Being a Distance Grandparent* I devoted an early chapter to explaining 'how it is' being a Distance Son or Daughter. I wanted to introduce the folks back home to your world.

This chapter is doing the same in reverse. While this book is about what Distance Sons and Daughters are thinking, feeling and experiencing, this chapter delivers readers a small taste of what distance parents and grandparents are ruminating about from afar. In my master's research, I asked New Zealand seniors, 'How is distance grandparenting for you?' This is a mini version of my findings.

Illustration by Cath Brew
drawntoastory.com

Once a parent, always a parent

Despite the cuteness and importance of the grandparent/grandchild relationship, I have found, and experienced myself, that you never stop being a parent. Parental thoughts rarely wane, even once grandchildren arrive on the scene. When I wake each morning, I first wonder how my *children* are, before I think about how my *grandchildren* are. In short, once a parent, always a parent.

The 'place' of distance grandparenting is multi-sited

At any one time, subject to resources and ability, we may find distance parents/grandparents performing their role in one of four places.

1. Their empty home - a place of mundane, comforting routines, but always with its spare bedroom or bedrooms unoccupied for long periods of time.
2. Their full home when hosting the Distance Family - invaded by an excited, boisterous cacophony of chatter and suitcases and all infused by a jet lag haze.
3. The full home of the Distance Son or Daughter when visited by the distance grandparents - both familiar and strange, with a décor backdrop that's normally only seen on a screen.
4. The virtual, digital, co-presence of cyberspace - a space that is frequently occupied during a pandemic.

Aloneness is ever-present

The thoughts and emotions of distance parents/grandparents are experienced in a quiet void that is a place of aloneness. They have little to show for this part of their being other than photos and trinkets about their home. There are no car seats in their vehicles, no familiar cars that come and go in the driveway and no toy corner in the sitting room.

Alone time - the greatest gift

Distance Family communication tends to be dominated by group video calls with all the family present. These occasions are always well received but what is missing are the one-on-one connections. Distance parents/grandparents value conversations when they have a family member all to themselves. There is an intimacy in something like a drive together in a car that can't be duplicated.

The in-country family matter

Siblings who remain in-country are the unsung heroes of Distance Families and deserve a moment of glory. I will revisit this topic later in the book.

Change is a constant companion

Distance grandparenting evolves, flip-flops and transitions as life and whatever the world throws at it causes constant change to grandparents' emotions and how they conduct their role. One day the entire distance thing doesn't feel so bad, and then something happens to the family on the other side of the world and they're in the depths of despair.

Acceptance

The invisible thread that connects these themes is acceptance - gracious acceptance by the parents/grandparents of the move their family has made. Does this come easy? Is this what they want? The answer, of course, is no. However, distance parents need to remember that when they brought up their children, they probably said "you can do anything" - and that's exactly what they've done. It just so happens it involves living somewhere else in the world.

Distance parents and grandparents adjust and accept on their own timetable. It is nearly always a two steps forward, one step back grieving/adjusting process. As the years pass, most get used to their situation and try to make the most of it.

Reflection

Many distance grandparents reflected with me about how, decades ago, *they* moved away from their parents to live in another city or country. Sometimes this is forgotten in the mix. Just like today's mobile generation, *they* were pulled to 'the big smoke', adventure or a more comfortable life on the other side of the world.

It never occurred to them that their parents might be upset. Society didn't have a rule decreeing this as a responsibility. Likewise, their parents didn't display their grief. It wasn't the done thing. Parents just got on with it, in the same way they'd witnessed their own parents watch family go to war. On the flip side there was no obligation for the same left-behind parents to 'be there' at the other end of the country or the other side of the world - to help, for example, when a grandchild was born.

2. UNPACKING DISTANCE SONS AND DAUGHTERS

"Some people are just born with itchy feet and a greater sense of adventure; they want to see the world and don't feel quite sure where they might eventually call 'home'."
Carole Hallett Mobbs, expat life mentor

Living and working overseas is nothing new. Past generations have emigrated, travelling by ship and rarely visiting 'home'. Their departure was like a funeral for the left-behind family. Then came the Big OE (Overseas Experience) or working holiday as I described earlier. In recent decades the gap year has become a contemporary rite of passage, when students take a break between studies to 'see the world'.

These there-and-back phenomena still exist, but contemporary global citizens, the subjects of this book, are seeking semi-permanent or permanent career-focused overseas employment, and their 'packages' aren't all the same.

In this chapter I outline the framework of contemporary expats and migrants because many aspects affect how they 'distance family'.

The Push and the Pull

Sociologists and historians differentiate between 'push factors' (reasons people emigrate, for example, war or economic depression) and 'pull factors' (reasons people immigrate to a specific country, for instance, employment opportunities). Pull factors dominate decision-making processes for most of the Distance Sons and Daughters featured in this book.

Here are some pull examples - more than one may apply:

- Study
- Career/job
- Love
- Challenge/adventure
- Freedom
- Quite simply, 'why not?'

The nature of the move/contract and how it can affect distance relationships

Even within 'pull factor' situations, Distance Sons and Daughters each have their own mobility story, and it affects intergenerational relationships and dynamics. In this book I tend to lump everyone in together, but there are distinct circumstances.

Let's address them:

A short-term, one-off overseas contract delivers one set of circumstances. Sometimes the Distance Son or Daughter relocates having searched out the role. Other times they have been recruited and the employer is assisting with the expense and formalities of the move. For all intents and purposes, they are returning home when the contract finishes.

The family back home sees this as an exciting family event and are consoled by the fact it is finite.

On-the-move, rotational, every-two-or-three-years expats are different again. These Distance Sons and Daughters are often from the corporate, diplomatic, military or missionary worlds. In most cases the moves are a choice; sometimes they're not. With each move, Distance Sons and Daughters get better at transitioning, making new friends, adjusting to the new culture and saying their goodbyes.

Initially, it's a novelty for all generations, including those at home. But in no time, continuous moves become the norm and there's a certain 'here we go again' that comes into play for everyone.

Nomadic lifestyles feature as well. I don't mean itinerant vagabonds here; I mean digitally savvy continent hoppers. Their physical home might be a series of geographically spread house-minding contracts that somehow or other align themselves to make this lifestyle a viable option. Or 'home' is a series of long-stay Airbnb contracts where the daily rate has been bargained down. All the while, the nomad's mobile/virtual business or job ticks along, providing a (hopefully) steady income to allow for this transient life choice.

Amy Scott has been on the move for much of her adult life and supports nomads via her *Nomadtopia* broadcasts. She explains that Distance Sons and Daughters who contemplate a nomadic lifestyle often do so in secret because naysayers who find the idea foreign to them will pour cold water upon their dreams. These critics include family members.

Settled in one place forever is a different package again. These Distance Sons and Daughters left home with a clear one-way directional plan or may have migrated across from one of the above categories to a more permanent situation. The folks back home accept that this is likely to be forever.

Rhoda Bangerter, Distance Daughter and author of *Holding the Fort Abroad*, explains that families can also hop from one category to another, and this can find them on the move, then semi-permanent, then back on the move again.

There are other factors that affect the nature of a move and how it impacts the wider family.

Location can matter because a cute township in rural Switzerland *feels* safer to some Distance Sons and Daughters compared to a developing nation with compromised medical facilities.

Location affects the willingness or feasibility of the Distance Family to visit. When my daughter and son-in-law lived in Pakistan, Clive and I were keen to visit, and they were keen to host. However, my family's employer wasn't prepared to accept responsibility for our personal safety in the event of an emergency. Our travel insurance company might also have had something to say, but we never got that far.

Where and when the grandchildren were born can, but not always, affect grandparent/grandchild relationships. There is a difference between having in-country grandchildren who move overseas when they are older and grandchildren who were born overseas so the grandparents have always been at a distance. When grandchildren can remember living in their passport country and regularly seeing their grandparents, there is a closeness that is harder to replicate from afar.

Multi-generational Distance Familying

A fair percentage of on-the-move expats are sons or daughters of parents who themselves lived overseas. Once you delve into the world of mobility, you soon discover multi-generational expat/migrant families - corporates, academics, military, missionaries, diplomats. Their parents were expats, they are expats and their children have experienced life living abroad. Each generation is following the other, which is a compliment to the earlier generation's lifestyle choices.

Is it any wonder that when these folk find themselves first-time distance grandparents, there's an element of under-the-breath, light-hearted déjà vu mutterings of "we got what we deserved"?

> "My parents [the distance grandparents] knew what to expect. They had been the middle generation of a three-generational expat family. They knew what they were

setting themselves up for when they took us overseas. When we were raised overseas, fuelling the fire of curiosity, this is the price they have to pay."

Anna Seidel (American Distance Daughter living in Germany)

Multi-generational Distance Families tend to have a higher level of robust emotional resilience. Life can still be hard, but they adjust and adapt more easily to their geographical separation. What is the norm for them can overwhelm some newer Distance Families.

Reflection

COVID-19 disrupted the theory of 'push' and 'pull'. On 16 March 2020, French President Emmanuel Macron addressed his nation. Six times he used the phrase "*Nous sommes en guerre*" [We are at war]. Wars change much. The 'pull' or attraction to leave home lost its sparkle for many potential departees. Existing expats and migrants were being 'pushed' home through choice or changing circumstances. I discuss this in more detail in *Chapters 19* and *23*.

3. UNPACKING EMOTIONS

"Mixed and contrasting emotions and feelings such as hope and nostalgia, guilt and ambition, affection and disaffection - to name but a few - are an integral part of the life experiences of migrants."
Sociologists Paolo Boccagni and Loretta Baldassar in *Emotion, Space and Society*

"I really enjoyed your podcast [Helen]. I started crying just reading the description of it... triggering an unknown grief (or is it guilt?) of my mum having to be a distance grandparent. Who knew those tears were there?!"
Anonymous contributor

"They [expats] focus all of their preparation on 30% of the move and either ignore or are woefully underprepared for the whopping 70%... if you truly want to thrive abroad, what you really need to prepare for are the emotional and mental aspects of your international move. Expat emotions like culture shock, homesickness, grief, uncertainty, and being away from loved ones, especially in the time of a global pandemic, can take a toll on you."
Mariam Navaid Ottimofiore, author of *This Messy Mobile Life*

After researching transnational families (Distance Families), Australian-based sociologist Zlatko Skrbiš concluded that emotions aren't a resource to *explain* Distance Family life, they are the *experience* in themselves. In other words, to 'do' Distance Families is to live in and be surrounded by emotion.

This chapter acknowledges the key emotions connected to the Distance Family role that expats and migrants quietly cope with, often in an alone space. They aren't discussed a lot with the folks back home but are centre stage for Distance Sons and Daughters. As author and researcher Rhoda Bangerter put it so well, these emotions are "something we rarely get to hear over the kitchen table when we visit [home], but we experience them first-hand, every day, as distance adult children".

Ambivalence and Ambiguity

"[Expats and migrants] experience millions of deaths of selves attached to places, friendships fallen by the wayside, missed opportunities and alternate realities."
Leigh Matthews, psychologist

Ambivalence and ambiguity are easily confused. Family therapist Pauline Boss from the Department of Social Science at the University of Minnesota offers a great explanation: "In the theory of ambiguous loss, ambivalence means conflicted emotions such as love and hate, whereas ambiguity means a lack of clarity... Ambiguous loss (in the relational sense) leads to ambivalence (in the social sense)."

Ambivalence is everywhere

Relationship ambivalence is experiencing both positive and negative feelings, or understandings of a situation, at the same time. Traditions, social expectations and social norms fuel it. Geographically close in-country family members experience ambivalence, so it is understandable that the Distance Family will also. Even the most dedicated, family-orientated Distance Son or Daughter experiences ambivalence within their Distance Family relationships - and that's okay.

Sociologist Dr Ingrid Arnet Connidis is a professor emerita at the University of Western Ontario, Canada. Her research focuses on family ties and relationships. She stresses that the analysis of ambivalence within families should be done on multiple levels. There are good days and bad days, good situations and bad situations, good years and bad years, good seasons and bad seasons. This applies to Distance Sons and Daughters navigating Distance Family relationships. It is an ever-changing kaleidoscope of contradictory, mixed-up, disrupted feelings and settled and unsettled situations. These all need to be considered.

Distance Sons and Daughters experience relief if they reach a plateau of 'business as normal' where ambivalence settles into a comfy, familiar groove. It is an excellent result.

What does all this mean? It is okay for Distance Sons and Daughters to experience ambivalence about their Distance Family. It is normal and understandable.

Ambiguous Loss

"The features of [ambiguous] loss in voluntary transnational families are different from families separated involuntarily."

Catherine Solheim and Jaime Ballard, mobility scholars

Pauline Boss coined the term 'ambiguous loss' in the 1970s. It's a loss that is unclear.

The separation loss for distance parents and grandparents is an involuntary loss. They didn't choose for their family to move away. Their loss is unclear because they haven't lost their children but those children are no longer around. The children are with them psychologically, but not physically.

There is an argument that says Distance Sons and Daughters do not 'qualify' as valid sufferers of ambiguous loss because, in most cases, the choice to leave was theirs. I argue that they do qualify.

Boss relayed the scenario of a young man who felt that losing his mobile phone was an ambiguous loss. When this story sits alongside those who Boss worked with, people who lost family members in catastrophic events such as 9/11 and the 2004 tsunami, the phone loss seems inconsequential. However, to this man, his phone was his 'life' and its loss was overwhelming and full of uncertainty. If he sees it as ambiguous, then it is, even if others don't see it that way.

If a Distance Son or Daughter experiences an unresolved loss, day in and day out, then for them that is an ambiguous loss, even if they have *chosen* to live where they live. Despite the purposeful circumstances, a loss is ever-present.

Ambiguous loss can be experienced by Distance Sons and Daughters because of:

- Uncertainty surrounding the length of an assignment
- One half of a couple deciding, or being forced, to opt out of traditional employment for all manner of reasons
- Concern over what could have been. What might the family have missed out on by opting for the life they have chosen?
- The 'loss' of a parent or grandparent affected by dementia
- More recently, COVID-19 generating ambiguous loss around the missed opportunities to travel, visit family and keep up connections

Distance parents and distance grandparents have *automatic* entry into the Ambiguous Loss Club. Distance Sons and Daughters, more often than not, end up as members because of circumstances that are beyond their control. It is important to realise that the folks back home probably don't think of it this way. They might say "but you chose to leave". But through understanding and empathy, they may come to appreciate that all generations can experience ambiguous loss.

Guilt Is a Constant Companion

"Guilt, guilt, guilt is what all migrants face."
Professor Loretta Baldassar

Psychotherapist and author of *Maybe You Should Talk to Someone* Lori Gottlieb says the following about guilt: "Guilt is useful if it tells us that we've gone against our own **internal moral code** and helps us make better choices next time. Guilt is crippling if it comes from the **'the outside'** and tells us that somebody else's ideas about how we should live are more important than our own... The minute you started to experience joy, you also experienced guilt. And the guilt won every single time."

When guilt is discussed in the context of Distance Familying, there are two types:

1. Guilt generated by you (Gottlieb's **internal moral code**). As clinical and health psychologist Melissa Parks admitted, she often asks herself, "Am I being the daughter I want to be?" This comes from a place of love, caring, empathy and knowing that *you* decided to live abroad.
2. Guilt imposed upon you (Gottlieb's **'the outside'**). This guilt is from others and comes from their place of grief,

disappointment and heartache. I would also add it can come from ignorance and, to some degree, selfishness on the part of your family back home.

Guilt generated by you

The bad news is it comes with the territory. I'm not going to list all the reasons why you experience guilt. You already know them, and you don't need to be reminded. I suggest you see guilt as an emotion you own - because you care. This is an admirable quality. The world would be an amazing place if it was full of caring people like you. If you didn't give a **** about your family, then that wouldn't be ideal.

It is also healthy to know that even in families where Distance Family members are accepting of your move, guilt still finds a home. Australian Distance Daughter Tanya Crossman has lived most of her adult life abroad and enjoys this luxury, but she still admits to experiencing guilt.

> "Knowing that I can only blame myself. That I'm the one who decided to go. That I could be closer but chose not to be. Knowing I valued something more highly than being near the family members I love so dearly. That's a hard truth to face - and yet also a hard one to escape!... I think the guilt can be like homesickness - coming in waves, rather than constant, sometimes taking you by surprise."
>
> Tanya Crossman (Distance Daughter)

Likewise, my husband and I are very accepting of our geographically dispersed family, but that doesn't mean our kids don't feel pangs of guilt when they think about how little time we spend together and the magic grandchild moments we miss out on.

Carole Hallett Mobbs, an expat life mentor and consultant, reminds us that guilt for Distance Sons and Daughters doesn't stop with the left-behind family. There's the guilt of children who may not settle well or who are struggling with schooling and/or a new language and just plain missing their grandparents. If you're a parent, at home or abroad, guilt is ever-present.

Guilt imposed upon you

This is real and too often showered upon Distance Sons and Daughters by those who love them the most. The emotions of your distance parents, grandparents and friends are not your responsibility, but while that's fine in theory, it's easier said than done.

The 3 H's - Language of Progressive Acceptance of Distance Grandparenting

Level One - Harmful

"How dare you take my grandchild to the other side of the world. What is wrong with this country? Do we not have any say in your decision?"

A natural response, but likely destructive. Those words are never forgotten.

Level Two - Human

"I miss you so much. I can feel the distance. I just want to be there and give you all a hug. I wish you could come home."

Honest, understandable and still best shared with friends.

Level Three - Helpful

"This is your decision and I respect your choices. I am proud of you and will keep loving and supporting you from afar."

Wisdom that will reap benefits.

The guilt imposed on Distance Sons and Daughters is reflected in the language of their parents and grandparents. In *Being a Distance Grandparent*, I talk frankly about the less than helpful language they sometimes use when communicating with their family from afar. I call it *The 3 H's*: the Language of Progressive Acceptance. As they grow in their acceptance of their situation, their language improves.

Distance parents and grandparents who've read *The 3 H's* have commented along the lines of "I needed to read this" or "I'm Level Two and that's not helping".

A sad by-product of having parents who shower Distance Sons and Daughters with guilt is that you share less with them. Your actions are understandable because it's all too hard. But as a result, distance parents and grandparents end up 'out of the loop' about what's going on, and most times, they don't know why.

Homesickness

"You will be a perpetual foreigner, someone whose heart belongs to different lands and different people, different versions of yourself... The muted yearning will never go away. Some days barely ache; others are filled with breathtaking pain. A pain I have to get used to, because if I left and went back to that land that still calls me, there I would just yearn and suffer for this one."

Melissa Meza-Rapp, contributor to *Somewhere: Women's Stories of Migration*

Tanya Crossman talks of homesickness "coming in waves". This reminds me of a tide calendar. When you live in a country like

New Zealand surrounded by oceans, a tide calendar is a commonly pinned item on a kitchen noticeboard.

Tidal movements are predictable when you keep an eye on the calendar. If you visit the beach and haven't checked the calendar, that broad stretch of sand you were hoping for could well be underwater. Homesickness is like this. It can come in predictable waves and patterns, but when you haven't thought about it for a while or something unexpected transports your brain thousands of miles away, just like a spontaneous visit to the beach, the tides (or emotions) can take you by surprise.

Another angle comes from anthropologists Mikkel Bille, Frida Hastrup and Tim Flohr Sørensen, who write about 'An Anthropology of Absence'. Their overriding message is that what is missing is just as important as what is there. As they explain, "People's engagement with the world does not simply consist in deducing the meaning of people, places and things or what they represent, but also in *presencing* that which is absent in one way or another." Homesickness is the presence of what is absent in one way or another.

> **"Homesickness is the presence of what is absent in one way or another."**

The senses have a lot to answer for

A whiff of a familiar meal in a marketplace, the taste of a favourite food from home, a strange but familiar accent heard in a crowd, the sight of a familiar flag in an unexpected place and the feel of a handwritten letter received in the mail; all of these can trigger homesickness. They elicit feelings of belonging to somewhere far off.

When I was young my mother would cook a roast dinner every weekend. The ritual was divine and as children we never bored of it. Years later, when I was a Distance Daughter in London, a friend had an oven - a prized amenity rarely found in budget 'digs' - and he invited us over for a roast lamb meal. Decades later my mouth still salivates when I recall us all sitting on the bed with plates on our laps and that oh so familiar smell and taste transporting me home. That roast dinner boosted me for weeks - at a time when Maggie Thatcher ruled with an iron fist and life was pretty tough.

I'll finish with more lyrical words from Melissa Meza-Rapp: "I am bound by bonds that can't be broken to that land, those people, the streets I walked on to go to school when I was 15, the sound and smells of the countries that I can't forget, that I don't want to forget."

Reflection

When researching for this book, it was hard to ignore an article titled 'Why Gratitude is the Best Answer for Difficult Expat Emotions'. The author, Jodi Harris, has 20 years' experience in social work, teaching, conflict management, mindfulness and global coaching. She's worked with every type of migrant or expat you can imagine. Jodi explains, "Learning to engage with gratitude provides unique ways in which to deal with many of the difficult emotions that plague our unpredictable international lives - so that we can always feel exactly the way we want to feel, but so that we can better address the very real emotions that sometimes knock us flat... If you're feeling helplessness, sadness, envy, anger, rejection or grief, it can be helpful to process those emotions by seeing them as part of your complex life - a life that also includes good things... even good things directly related to the challenges you're facing."

I'm a great believer in gratitude, and those who know me will confirm I tend to look on the bright side wherever possible. I'm not resentful that my children and grandchildren live overseas. I'm grateful they are safe, well and leading full lives.

4. DON'T ASSUME DISTANCE FAMILYING IS AUTOMATICALLY BAD NEWS

When my children were small and fell or hurt themselves, I would often chuckle rather than offer immediate sympathy. They would look at me in a confused manner, and most of the time, they'd just pick themselves up and brush themselves off. There wasn't a lot of drama. I took the attitude, it's only a problem when it's a problem. Distance Familying is exactly the same.

This is a short chapter with a very important message.

It is all too easy to assume that moving abroad will automatically be bad news for family relationships. Hand on heart, I can tell you that Distance Sons and Daughters and their children *can* have close relationships with their distance parents, grandparents and extended family. A geographical move doesn't have to be an automatic family disaster.

> **"Hand on heart, I can tell you that Distance Sons and Daughters and their children can have close relationships with their distance parents, grandparents and extended family. A geographical move doesn't have to be an automatic family disaster."**

I know this because I see and hear it time and time again. I have met many distance parents and grandparents who proudly report that they are closest to the ones who live the furthest away. Why? Because all parties, often led by intentional Distance Sons and Daughters, perform champion efforts to connect - and it works. Never feel that geographical separation will cause you to be distant. It doesn't have to be that way.

> **"Never feel that geographical separation will cause you to be distant. It doesn't have to be that way."**

Many parents and grandparents are accepting of their middle generation's move. Maybe not at first, but in time. The distance parents might even be half expecting the news when you tell them you're moving abroad. They probably have friends in the same situation. Distance parenting/grandparenting has become a social norm.

Your move creates a new dynamic within the family and a reason for parents/grandparents to travel and experience another world. This gives an adventuresome purpose to their retirement years, which is both healthy and exciting.

5. BEFORE YOU LEAVE

"When you hug them goodbye,
hold it for just a little bit longer."
Jerry Jones, global coach

In this chapter I discuss 'how it is' for sons and daughters when they are considering a move abroad. It's perfectly natural for your thinking space to be dominated by the urgent and the immediate, particularly if you're at the planning stage. But how do you support family relationships in the long term? The suggestions offered here are aimed at helping you 'leave well' - or at least as well as you can manage.

The Decision with a Capital D

The first sentence in *Expat Partner*, a career-focused mobility book by Carine Bormans and Marie Geukens, is: "What would it be like to live and work in another country?" I would add: "What would it be like to live away from my family?"

For most Distance Sons and Daughters, this is where it begins. A simple question with huge ramifications. They have a choice to live in their home country or live somewhere else - and they've simply chosen the latter. By the time their parents learn about the potential move, the middle generation is usually some way down the track - past the point of no return.

"How Dare You Take Our Grandchildren to the Other Side of the World. Don't We Have a Say in This?"

Distance Sons and Daughters are often afraid to tell their parents that they are on the move. They dread the conversation. If you're reading this as a potential expat or emigrant, you have a once-only opportunity to put in place, before you leave, a few things that will make a huge difference down the track.

Maria Marchetti-Mercer is a professor of psychology in South Africa - a country with prolific emigration. She's an advocate for those left behind in the migration narrative. Marchetti-Mercer stresses that much can be done, before leaving, to reduce the psychological impact on all parties. As she explains, "Those who plan to emigrate understandably tend to focus on the logistical and practical demands associated with leaving and finding a new home in an unfamiliar country. As a result they often tend to overlook proper psychological preparation nor sufficiently take into account how different members of the family will be impacted by this massive decision." She also goes as far as saying, "Grandparents often lose part of their identity as the elders in the family through the emigration of their children."

Here is a checklist for those *considering* moving abroad. Your actions will reap dividends, or at least reduce upset later on.

1. Ensure as husband/wife/partners you are secure and 'on the same page' about as much as possible, especially when it comes to how you'll treat and connect with your family. You'll be tested.

2. There are two trains of thought about when to tell parents/ grandparents about a move. If you're young and single heading off into the blue yonder, timing isn't so crucial; your parents are more than likely going to cope and accept

the plans pretty well. For established couples and family packages, I recommend telling parents/grandparents earlier rather than later about a potential move. I recall a podcast conversation with a South African relocation expert. We were discussing this dilemma and in jest he joked about ringing "the mother-in-law" from Johannesburg Airport to tell her he was off. I recommend against having everything organised and then springing it on them. Parents and grandparents will never forgive you, even if they don't verbalise their upset. As soon as there is a speck of an idea, speak up. Allow parents time to adjust. If the move doesn't go ahead, respect has been earned for involving the parents/grandparents.

3. Ensure distance parents/grandparents are conversant with technology. Be super patient and prepared to explain the same thing six times. Distance Sons and Daughters can fix problems remotely via screen sharing software like TeamViewer. Do practice runs ahead of your departure so the parents understand how they have to log on and advise their son or daughter of a password each time help is required.
4. Think about the time zone difference each generation will have to cope with after the move. Imagine the likely time of day and the day/s of the week you'll end up connecting once you've gone. Gently kickstart video calls between each other before the real thing - at the local 'home' time. These efforts will soon form a new and familiar rhythm to their day or week and won't feel so foreign once you leave.
5. If you have children, explain to them that they have a crucial role to play. As the saying goes, delegate, delegate. Encourage them to be regular initiators of one-on-one calls with their grandparents. Start before you leave. Because they already know their grandparents, your children are in a powerful position to help maintain relationships. They know the nooks and crannies of their house, which will become

the backdrop for future video calls. It's much tougher for children born overseas to establish the same familiarity. The other side to the grandchildren's narrative is that 'kids are kids'. Despite best intentions, there'll be times when children and teenagers won't have the space for talking with Grandma or Grandad. Distance Sons and Daughters and the folks back home need to recognise this.

6. Left-behind siblings are one of the greatest assets that departing Distance Sons and Daughters have, and it's wise to treat them well. Your move is not of their making and they'll be wondering about increased responsibilities once you're gone. Best not take them for granted. Acknowledge the situation with grace, keep them in the loop about how you're preparing your folks and tell them about the systems you're putting in place.
7. Departing sons and daughters shouldn't make promises they can't be sure are deliverable. As an example, if you offer to ring home every day, it will be difficult to keep up. Work on once a week, then anything more is a bonus.
8. Write a note to your parents and/or grandparents thanking them for their understanding and post it on the way to the airport. When parents/grandparents later struggle with the new void, they'll re-read the note and be reminded of how much their love, support and acceptance is appreciated. They'll never throw that letter away. One day, when they've passed on and it's time to sort their papers, the envelope will appear.

Robyn Vogels is South African and left her homeland 27 years ago. She has lived in many countries, and for the last 13 years, Melbourne, Australia, has been home. Robyn is a relocation professional who supports new migrants from the likes of South Africa and the U.S.A. into Australia. She is also a co-author of *Your*

D.I.Y. Move Guide to Australia. Robyn recommends preparing the parents and grandparents and stresses the value in supporting the children. There is an entire chapter in her book on the subject, and even if Australia isn't the destination, much of her advice still applies. One of Robyn's top tips is to arrange a family weekend a few months after arriving. As the authors say, "You need to regroup after a move and just relax around each other again. It is important, and we really wish everybody would consider this."

Reflection

I remember the time my daughter Lucy, who was single at the time, arrived in the ancient Swedish university town of Uppsala for a university exchange. Prior to this she had been on an 'off the grid' pilgrimage through Europe for several weeks. It was before the days of international mobile phones and easy texting back home. I felt sure that as soon as Lucy landed in Uppsala, and knowing she hadn't connected with home in weeks, sending some sort of message to her parents would be an absolute priority. When nothing arrived, I went from my normal composed self to a distracted, anxious parent. Amongst the left-behind paperwork was the phone number of a local Swedish student who was to be Lucy's settling in 'buddy'. I rang this poor fellow. What a panic merchant I was. Of course, Lucy was fine. In fact, within a fortnight, she had arranged for her one-semester exchange to become two, and she stayed on for the winter.

The reason I tell this story is that when Distance Sons and Daughters first arrive at their new destination, they have so many things to cope with. In the meantime, the folks back home can be at their most vulnerable - like I was. To save a lot of grief, there's wisdom in sending a brief email or text upon arrival that promises a fuller follow-up in a few days. By doing so, Distance Sons and

Daughters buy themselves a period of grace and reduce anxiety levels at home.

Distance Sons and Daughters leave home for the *first* time, just once. Handled well, this transition creates a sound foundation for a well-functioning Distance Family.

6. SETTLING IN

"Living apart can give rise to a greater freedom and autonomy, as well as opportunities to negotiate obligations and reconfigure familiar relations."
Leslie E Fesenmyer, anthropologist

This chapter acknowledges that much is new after a move, especially during the early days. There is no denying that such issues dominate the lives of expats and migrants. When they become problematic, these issues can swallow up every ounce of energy, making it extra hard to be an engaging, intentional Distance Son or Daughter. A glass of wine, a Netflix binge and an early night can feel far more appealing than putting on a cheery, positive face and ringing home.

Living in a Diaspora

Wikipedia defines a diaspora as a scattered population whose origin lies in a separate geographic locale. Historically, the word diaspora was used to refer to the mass dispersion of a population from its indigenous territories, specifically the dispersion of Jews.

New Zealand demographer Professor Paul Spoonley points out that the average diaspora size of OECD nations (native-born persons living abroad compared to the native population of the country) is 4.1% of the total population. New Zealand, however, sits at 14%, close to Portugal at 15.4% and Ireland at 17.4%. In contrast, the Australian diaspora is only 3% of its population.

These are interesting statistics to ponder on as they relate directly to the percentage of 'left-behind' families. Distance Familying is therefore more commonplace among the Portuguese, Irish and New Zealanders.

Depending on *where* Distance Sons and Daughters settle, their diaspora might be large or they might be the only American, Canadian, Australian (and so on) in the neighbourhood. This may excite some if they crave diversity, while others may feel incredibly alone.

During a visit to Atlanta, Georgia, to see my daughter, we spied a New Zealand flag flying outside a cute neighbourhood cottage. Lucy didn't know a single New Zealander in this city of just under six million people. We both stopped in our tracks and looked at each other. "Should we knock on the door and say hi?" We didn't, but I always wonder if we should have. Lucy's diaspora may have doubled or trebled in size with the ring of a doorbell. *Her* migrant experience, and that of others like her, differs vastly from a Distance Daughter living in an expat compound or Western-dominated apartment complex in the likes of Singapore or Dubai.

Housing

Deciding where to live in an unfamiliar location is a complex minefield:

- Rent or buy?
- Furnished or unfurnished?
- Apartment, house or compound community?
- Convenient for jobs, schools, amenities and/or public transport?
- Will a car/parking/garage be essential?
- Drive on the left, drive on the right or drive at all?

Some migrants and expats enjoy the benefit of a relocation agent, appointed and paid for by their employer. These professionals are like angels sent from heaven as they do much of the legwork around housing, schooling and much more. They willingly answer endless questions. However, in most respects, the majority of Distance Sons and Daughters are 'on their own', making a myriad of crucial decisions and hoping for the best.

For Distance Sons and Daughters, there is an additional dilemma. Should they pay a premium for a house or apartment with an additional bedroom for visiting family and friends, or might they deliberately steer away from that option (not necessarily because of the expense)? There are pros and cons on both sides. At the end of the day, they need to do what's right for them.

Children's Schooling

For some Distance Sons and Daughters, directions and choices about their children's education are reasonably straightforward. As an example, if the family is permanently migrating, younger children might automatically go to the local school down the road. As these children become teenagers and young adults, the path they take is much the same as their peers.

For other Distance Sons and Daughters, especially those who are constantly on the move, choices are anything but straightforward. Each location offers different solutions.

No matter what choices are made, knotty intergenerational family discussions can act out across continents; education comes with diverse cultural, societal and familial expectations.

Natasha Winnard is English and has a background in teaching. She lives in Rio de Janeiro, Brazil, with her husband and son. Natasha is an expert in global education and owns a consultancy business, assisting parents and their children to navigate the perils of education pathways. During a conversation, we bounced ideas off each other about the many scenarios that play out for Distance Sons and Daughters:

- Some cultures have a strong tradition of viewing it as essential that children attend 'the best' university back in their home country. They maintain it will improve the child's employment and career prospects. This is a particularly dominant factor in the U.S.A. (Ivy League) and the U.K. (Russell Group Universities).
- A child accustomed to mixing in global circles often finds attending university 'back home' rather suffocating if it's a monocultural society. They yearn for a culturally rich environment, and universities back home are sometimes shunned in favour of a foreign university somewhere else. External factors can also affect choice. For example, Brexit narrowed university choice for U.K. citizens looking to study in the EU. Internationally, temporary border closures due to COVID-19 did the same.
- The pressure to achieve the required university entry results may appear, to some extended family members, to be completely over-the-top. This is part of an actual conversation: "You [distance grandparents] can't visit in August because that's when GCE results arrive, and we'll all be very stressed."
- Some cultures have a strong tradition of grandparents expecting to and/or offering to financially support grandchildren's secondary and/or university education. When one set of grandparents supports the cause and it's a completely foreign concept to the other grandparents, the outcome can be problematic.
- Teenagers are sometimes sent to boarding school back home for the last couple of years of their secondary education so

they later qualify for ongoing 'local' university fee levels and aren't treated as an international student.

- Young adults are sometimes sent to university back home to live with their grandparents. The middle generation often has a romantic idea that this will be a wonderful arrangement, while in fact, the grandparents find being 'responsible' for their grandchild quite overwhelming. They've always been the fun grandparents and now they have to be like parents. The transition can be especially tough if the child has been accustomed to domestic help and isn't used to contributing to everyday household tasks.

Intergenerational families who harmoniously and successfully navigate these situations are the exception to the rule. It all comes down to having brutally honest, ideally face-to-face, conversations.

For a deeper understanding of the migrant/expat schooling dilemma, I recommend *A Parent's Guide to Raising Kids Overseas* by international school psychologist Jeff Devens. His steady advice delivers parents and interested Distance Family members certainty about how to navigate children's education.

Domestic Help

In some destinations, employing domestic help is the norm. For most Distance Sons and Daughters it comes with confused and conflicting emotions. Those raised with little or no home-help struggle, knowing that these people are paid low rates and come from less than ideal, sometimes precarious, personal situations.

I have some first-hand experience of this. My daughter and her husband employed a nanny/housekeeper when they lived in Bangkok. Just like my daughter, I felt awkward during visits when the housekeeper 'did' for us all. I'm not one for lounging around, and she would jokingly tell me off when she arrived to find the breakfast dishes already done. In time, I learnt that Westerners are expected to hire staff; it's a way of contributing to the country's economy. My daughter and son-in-law made a point of paying their home-helps above the going rate and were constantly concerned about their well-being. When they moved to the States and had to say goodbye to a Filipino nanny who had lovingly cared for my little grandson, tears flowed freely - even from my tough-on-the-outside ex-military son-in-law. Years later, I still see that nanny saying 'hi' on Facebook and sending messages of love to my grandsons. I am grateful for the impact she had on our family.

> "We lived in China and South Africa and had domestic help - lovely - and I miss them dearly, but when we came here [Germany] it was clear that we were going to be doing it all again ourselves. So I told the kids from Day 1, before we got here, you are going to learn to empty a dishwasher and fold your laundry and clean your bathroom. This is a non-negotiable. They have to do it."
>
> Anna Seidel (American Distance Daughter in Germany)

The New Job

New jobs and careers feature in *Chapter 7*. They are clearly very important to Distance Sons and Daughters and are often the reason for the move.

The intergenerational experience can vary for the folks back home depending on whether it is *their* son or daughter who heads to work first. One will be more available than the other, and that affects their ability to connect.

Likewise, it's unlikely that a Distance Son or Daughter will come home from the first day of their new job and share with their folks back home everything they have gleaned about the vastly different work culture, systems, hierarchy and expectations. It's a tough and lonely space and one they navigate by themselves.

'Holding the Fort Abroad'

Many expats and migrants travel extensively with their jobs, and I have 'borrowed' this title. Rhoda Bangerter is a Distance Daughter and fellow author. *Holding the Fort Abroad* is the title of her book, a book that fills a vital gap on global mobility bookshelves. For 16 years Rhoda's husband worked away from home, including time in Kabul, Afghanistan, while she 'held the fort' in Switzerland (his home country, not hers) with their two boys. This resonated with me. For two years, a long time ago, I was a solo mother with two in diapers - an experience that gave me a real taste of what Rhoda had to cope with.

Jeff Devens offers a frank commentary on this topic. He explains, "I have met with scores of families arriving overseas for their first posting or deployment that did not realize the demands that would be placed on the working spouse and, subsequently, the family."

Being separated and living in countries where you are also a foreigner is a tough gig. It requires expat/migrant superpowers. These demands naturally put pressure on keeping up connections with the Distance Family. Rhoda's book can launch precious conversations, and I recommend couples own a copy each.

If you are a distance parent or grandparent, let me share some advice Rhoda passed on to me. "Be aware of the amount of work travel that is involved in your son's/daughter's life or their partner's life. If you call when their spouse is away, and it's been a few weeks of parenting alone, you may get a different response from if you call when the partner is home. They may need more support also: an encouraging note, or timing visits for when the travelling partner is away."

Reflection

As distance parents and grandparents, we'll never truly appreciate how it feels for our children to land in a new city, in a foreign country. How daunting it must be to deliver children to a school that is vastly different to anything they've experienced themselves, hoping their brave offspring will understand the accents, languages and new ways of doing things. The settling-in journey is definitely one that is theirs alone, and the Distance Family are observers from afar. By the time we turn up, our children have smoothed out most of the wrinkles and life is on cruise control, even if the motorway still feels unfamiliar. It's a huge achievement.

7. NAVIGATING WORK

"Both globalization and dual income couples... are on the increase throughout the world. Even in countries like Japan, where numbers have been historically lower, they are now on the rise. Managing two careers across borders increases both the complexity and the challenges for both partners."
Yvonne Quahe, *Whose Career - Yours, Mine or Ours?*

Today's Distance Sons and Daughters, many of them part of the Gen X and Gen Y/Millennial cohorts, are some of the most educated in history. In general, their Baby Boomer parents had fewer educational opportunities and their gender roles were - and often remain - more defined.

Highly educated expats/migrants are in high demand and frequently choose where they move to. The by-product of this higher education and all it took in time, energy and money is that career paths and professional development have become of paramount importance. Most are looking out for the next move: the next advancing opportunity.

'Settled' in one place migrant couples and on-the-move expats have similar and dissimilar work/career-related experiences. Issues of employment (or lack of it) do not directly affect the role of being a Distance Son or Daughter. However, when jobs are overly demanding and/or require extensive travel, this can take its toll and affect how Distance Sons and Daughters maintain relationships back home.

Understanding the experiences of those abroad is important; it creates empathy. And as we know, empathy is a good thing for all Distance Families.

Starting a Family

Though it is usually a welcomed milestone, impending parenthood can upset career plans. Financial strains, gender role inequality and identity issues take centre stage as the parents are raising their child or children.

In a podcast, First Lady Michelle Obama said that when she talked to mothers, it was all about "How do I have it all?... And how do you get it? And if you're not getting it then something is wrong". Life has taught these mothers that they should be able to have it all. But when you throw in cultural differences and social norms that vary from country to country, having it all can be difficult.

Impending parenthood can generate inappropriate messages from home that it's time to return. Be swift and firm in your response so there is no chance of these unwelcome pleas gathering momentum.

The Expat/Migrant *Partner* Experience

'Settled' migrant couples tend to live where *both* can work, plus they have the luxury of knowing they have time on their side to work on careers and home life plans as they won't be moving again any time soon.

In contrast, when an on-the-move expat couple or family relocates due to the career prospects of *one* half of the couple, frequently the other half cannot obtain a work visa. Corporate, military, missionary, diplomatic and NGO on-the-move assignments can end up with this type of scenario. The non-employed other half (usually the woman) often feels rudderless and asks themselves, "What am I going to do and how much time have I got to do it before we're on the move again?" They're not able to grow their career - do something for them - and their identity takes a battering. Marcela, a contributing essay writing student in Diane Comer's *The Braided River*, described her supporting partner experience as "a side dish to the main course".

For the first few weeks of relocation it doesn't matter too much as there are so many things to get sorted, and it's a bonus if one half of a couple can take charge on the home front and both aren't expected to turn up at the office bright and cheerful on Monday morning. The couple becomes a team, each doing what needs to be done, and that's a temporary positive.

In time, though, this busyness calms down and thoughts about making a mark, using their education and qualifications, climbing the career ladder and not being left behind are uppermost in their minds. For the 'unproductive' spouse who is yearning to get back into the workforce and gain a sense of purpose and identity, the visa and/or language restraints make it feel like they're treading water.

If you're a Distance Family member reading this and have a Distance Son or Daughter who is 'keeping the home fires burning', you can be pretty sure they're finding the situation massively frustrating, even if they're not telling you.

There is help!

In their book *Expat Partner* Carine Bormans and Marie Geukens are sympathetic to and have a positive attitude towards the dilemma of the partner spouse. The theme of their findings is that each posting can come with different priorities for the expat partners to focus on and it's wise to stand back and reflect on these. Rather than seeing a set of circumstances as restrictive - not having the right visa to chase employment, for instance - it's possible to turn the circumstances around, change expectations and see this as a posting with other priorities. As they say, there are multiple solutions for multiple situations, and keeping an open mind to other ways of achieving professional development is key.

Yvonne Quahe is an author friend and distance grandmother. Importantly for this topic, she is also a sociologist, coach and HR professional. Yvonne's book is called *Whose Career - Yours, Mine or Ours?* Great question. My biggest take from her book and from our conversations is that so few migrant/expat couples talk about how, as a team, they will navigate their two career paths. Over and over she has met couples where one half is resentful that their career has been put on hold while they're forced to follow a partner who is sometimes oblivious. It doesn't help that many corporations barely acknowledge the partner spouse.

Moves around the world can seem, from the outside, a splendid adventure, but once the initial honeymoon period has petered out, reality sets in and it can be an enormous shock for the one who has followed.

I can't stress enough that this is a dynamic that needs to be understood - *before* considering a move. I would go as far as saying, if you're reading this and you're a soon-to-become distance parent/grandparent, I'd suggest gifting your son or daughter copies of these books. There isn't another topic (except expat guilt, maybe) that is more prolific in Distance Son and especially Distance Daughter circles.

Warrior Princes and Warrior Princesses

I need to give the credit for this topic title to a New Zealand distance grandmother friend. One day when we happened to be at the hairdresser together, sharing as women do, she talked about these terms using her England-based Distance Daughter as an example.

At the time, her daughter worked in the marketing arm of a global NGO. Even with a small baby in tow, she was bounding out of the door for high-powered meetings and events. She was always frenetically busy drumming up support, fundraising and doing whatever it took to promote the agency's agenda.

Communication such as video calls were tricky with her as she was time-poor. Shared family activities during U.K. visits took second place, and even when her daughter visited New Zealand, she was a whirlwind of activity that never went on pause.

Warrior Princes and Warrior Princesses are zealous Distance Sons and Daughters committed to good and honourable causes with the fervour of an evangelical preacher. They tend to work for charities, aid agencies and NGOs. Their daily activities overflow with valuable good works, going above and beyond their duty. There is very little downtime and relaxing holidays are rare. Some observers might say, or at least *like* to say, that these Warriors are workaholics. The 'guilty' middle generation are likely to say they love every minute of their work.

What is difficult for the extended family, near and far, is that this work is 'doing good' and it doesn't feel right to complain about the lack of attention they receive as a result, or about the disruption it causes in their shared lives. Let's face it, the world needs Warrior Princes and Warrior Princesses.

This group of Distance Sons and Daughters doesn't dominate the statistics, but are you one of them? Perhaps you're not sure. Your family could answer that question - if you asked them. They won't tell you themselves. I know for a fact that your distance parents love visits, but they're also likely to be relieved when one party or other is due to return home.

Am I saying don't do good deeds? Absolutely not. Distance Families feel a great sense of pride in the work of Warrior Princes and Princesses, but there is wisdom in acknowledging that extended family members pay the price twice over: the geographical distance and the passionate, time-poor fervour.

Reinvention: Be Wary of the Messages from Home

To reinvent yourself in expat/migrant life is to willingly, or by necessity, change careers or direction in life, searching out a new passion, job or way of feeling and being productive. Some Distance Sons and Daughters accept this move willingly, but others, thrown into a situation where so much of what they've known isn't possible or is no longer their preference, are more begrudging. They encourage themselves or receive encouragement and/or pressure from fellow expats and sometimes from those at home.

Values can be a motivator. For example, they may quit a stressful career job in favour of a values-based community project or cause, often on lower pay or as a volunteer. Likewise, creativity can be a dominant driving factor. They may become artists, artisans or writers.

Sara Coggiola is an Italian Distance Daughter living in Australia. In her work as a certified life coach with clients all around the world, she has developed a keen interest in reinvention and has searched out 'reinventors', establishing a podcast devoted to the subject. As Sara explains, reinvention can be troublesome: "Most reinventors are on a solo journey, metaphorically."

There are cultural factors that come into play, too, says Sara, and these affect the messages received from home. Many Americans, for example, are used to changing jobs and updating their competences, and women are often very ambitious. Americans tend to embrace reinvention with enthusiasm and excitement, and messages from home are positive. In Italy, reinvention sometimes occurs because of necessity and because of prejudices from all sides. Italian expats and migrants find themselves fighting with Distance Family members who insist on sharing their differing mindsets. Cheerleader messages from home are always preferable.

Retirement

Even deciding where to retire can be problematic for Distance Sons and Daughters. Do you go home to be close to elderly parents? Returning home can almost feel like you've lost the meaning and purpose of life. Your former 'away' world was full to the brim, and the relative quiet of home can be overwhelming. Then there are the questions about where your adult children will settle, and let's not forget issues of passports, visas, citizenship, pensions, medical benefits and so on. And so the cycle begins again. Retirement for Distance Sons and Daughters can be riddled with question marks.

Reflection

Thoughts on what Distance Sons and Daughters could or should do when it comes to careers and jobs can come from different head spaces. Our three Distance Children have experienced many changes over the years with their jobs and careers. Some of their thoughts and plans have made sense to us, while others have felt a tad precarious. Throughout, we have always made it our job to be their encouragers.

If you are a distance parent or grandparent reading this, I would encourage you to 'zip up' when career plans make no sense to you. Of course, if asked your opinion, say your piece, but if not, let it be. The world changes fast and we can't expect to know or understand all the contemporary nuances of career moves. It's hard enough for Distance Sons and Daughters to keep up, let alone distance parents, grandparents and extended family on the other side of the world.

Finally, Distance Sons and Daughters, I'm going to add something from the perspective of a Baby Boomer - because I am one. If one half of a couple can stay home - more or less - and 'be there' when the children are young, please don't see it as a worrisome gap in your CV. And if you need any convincing, don't listen to me, watch 7-year-old Molly Wright's TED Talk titled *How every child can thrive by five* at https://www.ted.com/talks/molly_wright_how_every_child_can_thrive_by_five.

8. IDENTITY AND THE MEANING OF HOME

"Even as migrants close the distance between self and other in the host country, they open up a distance between themselves and where they once lived. For them, negotiating these different forms of distance is an ongoing challenge."
Diane Comer, *The Braided River*

What does home mean for Distance Sons and Daughters?

- Home can mean a taste: ethnic dishes, mother's cooking, a favourite hard-to-buy confectionary item.
- Home can mean a smell: street vendors, a particular flower, a waft of Dad's cigar.
- Home can mean weather: rain, humidity, heat, blue sky, fresh air.
- Home can mean sensations: sand between your toes, the surround-sound comfy blanket sensation of familiar accents when flying with a national carrier.
- Home can mean sounds: a national anthem, birdsong, waves crashing, silence.

At first, a garish flag hanging out of a shared flat window in a budget part of town may visually represent home. Over time, perhaps it's replaced with a treasured piece of artisan artwork from home that co-ordinates with the décor. More than likely, the weather-worn flag hasn't been discarded: it's stored away in a box of precious memorabilia.

Transition and relocation coach Marianna Kisvardai says a good way of studying the question of home is to observe the language or vocabulary used by Distance Sons and Daughters. When talking with their local friends, 'home' is the apartment or house where they live. With their distance parents, there could be a casual reference to their 'away' residence as home, but in the next sentence, home is where their parents live: the place of their roots. Less enthusiastic expats/migrants may explain home with cynical hand signals showing virtual quotation marks, while others may use the clinical term, 'passport country'.

Home and identity... can be a part of your being

Home can represent a place-of-pride part of your identity - something that is precious to you. Let's head to my son in Chicago.

After the 2019 terrorist shootings in Christchurch, New Zealand, Robbie explained to me that his identity as a Kiwi living in America had changed overnight. He'd always claimed he was from a country "devoid of terrorism", a badge of honour he wore with pride. But now, for him, New Zealand was tainted. He grieved the New Zealand he'd always known and revered. Home for Robbie was now a "damaged" version of itself. Until he spoke up, no one at home, including me, had fully comprehended how it was for him at the time.

When you live in a society where home has always been home and most people around you are like you - as many distance parents, grandparents and extended family do - it is rare to think about your identity, because you blend in. It is a luxury those of us in that situation often take for granted.

Well-meaning but Irritating Questions

Being a Distance Son or Daughter means living with questions of identity, and the meaning of home permeates every moment of every day. The folks back home have little comprehension of this constant mental workout.

"Where are you from?"

As soon as Distance Sons and Daughters open their mouth anywhere that isn't home, they are on 'standby'. When a stranger hears their accent and/or assesses their looks, they're expecting the inevitable question: "Where are you from?" This can happen ordering a cup of coffee or, more concerningly, when they're counting the precious minutes allocated for a doctor's consultation. It's not always bad, but most of the time it's irritating and intrusive. Distance Sons and Daughters don't want to continually answer the "where are you from?" question because it's irrelevant to them; they just want to blend in. The luxury of blending in and living life in the locals' lane is constantly out of reach.

When the folks visit, they're not surprised to find themselves a 'foreign' novelty for a couple of weeks, but they have no idea what it's like to be a novelty all the time.

"Why on earth would you ever leave?"

Without meaning to boast, New Zealand is high on the list of best places to live, and there are other countries like ours that are viewed as fairly exotic.

If Distance Sons and Daughters leave one of these favoured countries, they have to justify to the locals *why* they left. It's tiresome and in some ways a personal imposition, even though they realise the locals are taking an interest in them.

My American-based daughter was asked to write an article on this very subject for her church bulletin. Americans constantly ask why she gave up all the breathtaking natural beauty, progressive social policies and entrepreneurial spirit of New Zealand. As she freely admits, she didn't flee persecution, war or conflict. She wasn't a refugee, asylum seeker or displaced person. "I was young and ambitious," she said, "listening to the Dixie Chicks' *Wide Open Spaces*. I had a hunger for the unknown." Like so many down under younger people, she wanted to experience the world.

These days she turns this question around to ask why she hasn't gone back. The answer is just as complicated and involves two children, co-parenting and a career path. For her, it's also about 'belonging' and community: the vital ingredients that all expats and migrants yearn for. Once achieved, the desire to stay is stronger than the desire to return.

Reflection

In defence of the distance parents and/or grandparents, they also have to cope with irritating questions. Well-meaning, intelligent and even well-travelled friends ask if or when the offspring are coming home. For example, my stepson Guy has lived in the U.K. for 30 years and has two English-born children, 19 and 22 years old. When his marriage broke up a couple of years ago, many of my local friends asked if he was "coming home". It was the last thing he was considering. The U.K. is his home. His family is there. His career is there, and he is a U.K. passport-carrying citizen. Similarly, when my daughter's marriage ended, people asked the same thing. She has a 50/50 co-parenting agreement with her U.S. citizen ex-husband, two very American boys and a life and career where she lives. So yes, Distance parents and grandparents also have to cope with irritating questions.

In some respects, parents and grandparents end up like ambassadors or PR specialists for their Distance Sons and Daughters. I'm always surprised how often I'm asked the *same* question over and over by the *same* person. If they don't have Distance Family themselves, they just don't get it. On the flip side, no extended explanations are required when chatting with friends who have family afar. Being on the same page really helps.

9. CULTURE AND LANGUAGE

"We tend to have a blind spot when it comes to understanding how we may be perceived by others. Nearly all of us are certain that what we do is 'normal' and that it's everyone else who is different, but of course that is how they see it too."
Patti McCarthy, author of *Cultural Chemistry*

Being a Distance Son or Daughter means living with, and accepting, cultural differences in every aspect of their lives, inside and outside of home. These could be big-deal considerations of who they marry or partner with, what language or languages their children are raised with or what religion/s (if any) they embrace. Then there are choices of food, what to wear, household help, money management, work-life balance, who they'll vote for (if they're entitled to vote), where they'll spend the likes of Christmas or Thanksgiving and who with, and whether Thanksgiving is important anyway. There are also old family beliefs, embedded traditions and newly gained cultural values: a daily minefield that can be exhausting and overwhelming to navigate.

Canadian scholars Senanu Kutor, Alexandru Raileanu and Dragos Simandan have a refreshing take on this in a joint *Migration Studies* article. They argue that "the experience of international migration and subsequent cross-cultural interaction can be usefully understood as a 'fertile ground' for the flourishing of personal wisdom, which itself can act as an individual and collective resource for cohabitation in multicultural settings". The folks and family back home have limited awareness of the demanding cultural workout that is navigated by Distance Sons and Daughters and, yes, the wisdom and perspective they gain.

A Clearer Sense of Self in the Global Arena

"The migrant sometimes feels like a stranger to herself as she recreates herself and her home, and clings to other aspects of her former life."
Lorna Jane Harvey, editor of *Somewhere: Women's Stories of Migration*

In fascinating research that was approached from all angles, a group of MBA students wanted to know if living abroad increases 'self-concept clarity'. They were 'foreign' students and that was *their* experience. Was it the same for others? They concluded: "When people live in their home country, they are often surrounded by others who mostly behave in similar ways, so they are not compelled to question whether their own behaviours reflect their core values or the values of the culture in which they are embedded. In contrast, when living abroad... people's exposure to novel cultural values and norms prompts them to repeatedly engage with their own values and beliefs, which are then either discarded or strengthened." This generates 'self-concept clarity' - an understanding of who you are as a person.

Their finding is crucial to this book's narrative. Distance Sons and Daughters change, grow and expand their thinking in ways that they would not have done, to the same degree, if they had stayed home.

"Distance Sons and Daughters change, grow and expand their thinking in ways that they would not have done, to the same degree, if they had stayed home."

This is not a criticism of people who stay home, but it does affect how Distance Sons and Daughters see themselves and their new world. There are some things they will always have in common with their family back home, but there will be aspects of their lives where there is little commonality.

There was an interesting additional finding from the students. They reported that the depth of international experiences (the total time lived abroad), not the breadth of international experiences (the number of countries lived in), contributed to this clearer sense of self. It could be tempting to think that on-the-move, every-two-or-three-years expats will achieve greater clarity than migrants who settle permanently. But the students' research found that this was not the case.

In the bigger picture of Distance Families, this confirms that Distance Sons and Daughters who enjoy international travel and exposure to other cultures as children potentially have a head start when it comes to feeling at home in the global arena.

Cultural Immersion

"If cultures are to meet rather than clash, we need to understand not just how others differ from ourselves, but how we differ from them."
Dr Julian Baggini, *How the World Thinks: A Global History of Philosophy*

Scholars talk of multiculturalism, affirmative philosophy, cultural assimilation and social integration. In simple terms, Distance Sons and Daughters learn to fast-track acquiring a sense of 'at homeness' in a new location. It's all about integration. New rules and cultural norms require bucketloads of curiosity, embracing differences and finding acceptance. Once achieved, all agree, life is enriched.

Culture shock

Potholes can litter the road to feeling at home in a new location. The experience is called culture shock, and few escape the loneliness it creates.

Lorna Jane Harvey, editor of *Somewhere: Women's Stories of Migration*, summed it up well: "The daily reality I encountered was a blend of a bit of everything: cultural mosaic, melting pot, acceptance, racism, social inequality, equal opportunity, traditions, distortion of national identity, rich culture, ethno-racial tensions, social and economic integration... My experience, for the most part, has been positive and enriching, but I see migrants... who struggle every day."

In *Chapter 19*, I explore *reverse* culture shock: when visiting home transitions from feeling like the old and familiar to a new, foreign version of itself. The lives of expats and migrants are filled to the brim with see-sawing cultural experiences that test their patience, emotional well-being, identity and sense of home.

Extended Family and Cultural Awareness

Sneha Jhanb, a contributor in *Raising the Global Mindset*, spoke frankly when she explained that it was normal for Distance Sons and Daughters to look to their parents for support. However, when multicultural parenting is part of the equation, the required support is also mental and emotional. "And sometimes," she says, "due to differences of opinions, the very support system that we look forward to becomes a hindrance."

Mariam Navaid Ottimofiore's book *This Messy Mobile Life* features a graph backing up Sneha's comment. It notes that the top three challenges are Race, Religion and Unresolved Grief. Fourth is "dealing with the cultural expectations from in-laws or relatives which differ from your own cross-cultural family". It takes courage for Distance Sons and Daughters to make decisions that sit with *their* values and not with those of extended family.

While Distance Sons and Daughters are working hard to blend in, say the right thing, eat the right food, nod, bow, shake hands, give the right gifts at the right time, how culturally in-tune are their distance parents, grandparents and other family (and friends) from afar when they visit?

Distance Sons and Daughters cope with a mixture of:

1. Cultural ignorance and inexperience displayed by the Distance Family
2. Cultural expectations from relatives that are hard to deliver

Intercultural competency enhances Distance Familying. As Sneha explains, "As much as it is the job of us [Distance Sons and Daughters] to understand our parents' point of view, it is that much more important for today's grandparents to understand their children." Some families achieve this organically and everyone is near enough on the same page, with just the odd, unintentional faux pas. Other families are oceans apart in their understanding. When an extended family member's cultural radar isn't well-tuned and they come up with inappropriate blunders and embarrassing comments, the guilty party is not even aware.

On a larger scale, whole nationalities can be out of tune with each other. In his confronting article 'Why Americans Die on Donuts while the French Thrive on Pastries', Dave Smurthwaite says: "In America, smoking is a moral issue, but over-eating is not. In Europe, over-eating is the big moral issue, not smoking."

Is it any wonder generational cultural awareness is a challenging goal? This can all be difficult for the Distance Son or Daughter, especially during visits when they're mixing outside of their home.

Australian-born Josephine O'Brien was raised on a farm in New South Wales and now lives abroad. In *Raising the Global Mindset*, she offers a balanced approach: "I grew up in a Christian household but at university met a group of friends that led me to Islam and my husband." Josephine converted to Islam and their children are raised in their shared faith. However, when they visit Australia, they join in with local festivals and religious feast days such as Easter and Christmas. "We explain [to their children] why we don't celebrate these days, but they are important to their grandparents so must be respected."

But We All Speak English

"Moving to another English-speaking country in many ways lulls people into a false sense of security: they confuse language with culture and imagine that because they use the same words, the meaning conveyed will be the same too."
Patti McCarthy, *Cultural Chemistry*

Patti is so right. Between them, our four Kiwi children married an English girl, an American girl, an Irish/American chap and a Scotsman. When we first met our American son-in-law, he addressed my husband as "Sir". We appreciated this respectful courtesy but assured him that in New Zealand we were far too informal for "Sir" and that "Clive" would be fine. Two of our grandchildren have cultured ('public school') English accents, two speak with a Southern American drawl and two have an unmistakable New Zealand twang. We might all speak English, for which I am most grateful, but for sure, there are subtle, and some not so subtle, cultural differences.

I remember an upcoming Christmas visit home from America where we had strict instructions to source particular 'holiday movie' DVDs. Sitting inside watching television on a summer's day was hardly normal at our end, but for our American son-in-law, Christmas didn't feel like Christmas without his favourite seasonal films. Once, when we were invited to dinner with friends in America, I offered to 'bring a plate' as we would say in New Zealand. I suggested a fruit salad as I thought I could manage to produce that from my basic Airbnb kitchen. I expected it to be served with ice cream, for dessert. Instead, it popped up as a side dish to the hamburger main course. Clive and I looked at each other and grinned. We went with the flow. On a trip to England one Christmas, we had no idea how important greetings cards were: everyone gave everyone a card on Christmas morning. A quick trip to the supermarket on Christmas Eve saved the day, but it was a close call.

Despite our shared language, English-speaking Distance Families still have to be on their toes - though some of these cultural misunderstandings are harmless and rather funny.

What Is the Language of Home?

"To be without the anchor of language is to be adrift in the world."
Diane Comer, *The Braided River*

When Distance Sons and Daughters partner with someone from a country that has a different language, it can raise some tricky questions. Which language will they choose as their 'home' language? Which one will their children speak? How will their choice affect their distance parents and grandparents (who may speak another language altogether)?

This topic reminds me again of the title of Yvonne Quahe's book about dual careers, *Whose Career - Yours, Mine or Ours?* Settling on which language/s to use in some Distance Son and Daughter households can be a case of yours, mine, ours, theirs, the school's or the language of their current location. And each of these languages can be different. Bilingual and multilingual expats who are on the move navigate many languages, with varying degrees of competency depending upon the context.

Of all the cultural adjustments within Distance Family generations, language is the one that can have the most far-reaching consequences: Distance Sons and Daughters can find themselves in continual damage control. Some of their Distance Family members are in awe at their ever-growing linguistic skills. Others feel lost and on the outer.

> "Our toddler grandson in Germany speaks four languages. We're blown away when we hear him."
>
> Fiona (New Zealand distance grandmother)

Some distance grandparents are critical and claim it is confusing for their grandchildren to be surrounded by multiple languages. Dr Ute Limacher-Riebold is an intercultural language and communication consultant. Dr Karin Martin is a linguist, lecturer and senior researcher/consultant for multilingualism. They passionately support parents and their children in bilingual and multilingual situations. Ute and Karin's message is that children are brilliant and deal with language confusion well. Children process what's important to understand *now*, and what they don't need they flush for the moment. For sure, they can get muddled along the way, but this cognitive workout is not only impressive, it's also beneficial for children's development.

Different languages across generations

"The ability to speak the native language is important because it allows children to communicate with their grandparents and extended family."
Olena Nesteruk and Loren Marks, 'Grandparents Across the Ocean', *Journal of Comparative Family Studies*

When the language of the grandparents differs from the primary language of their distance grandchildren, there can be issues. Most times, the grandchildren have a knowledge of their grandparents' language because at least one of their parents speaks it; however, how enthusiastically they embrace this language can vary. This is no reflection on them as members of a scattered family, or their Distance Son or Daughter parents. Sometimes it's simply 'kids are kids'. As Ute and Karin explain, children work on languages they see as important to them.

On another occasion Ute shared that it is possible for adults and children to relate acquired languages to parts of their body. For example, a child may think of one language as the language of their brain (for school learning). Another language might be the language of their feet (for watching soccer). A crucial question to ask is, what is the language of their heart? Which language represents their emotions? If this is not the same as the language spoken by their Distance Family, close connections are harder to achieve.

These situations can cause different outcomes:

- Grief for the grandparents, who feel a sense of disconnection, especially if they have little or no knowledge of their grandchildren's primary language

- Different levels of relationship closeness when grandchildren embrace their grandparents' language with varying levels of enthusiasm. An unevenness exists.
- Grief for the Distance Son or Distance Daughter who feels their mother tongue isn't part of their family's identity, or their own
- A lack of willingness to travel and visit each other because the language barrier makes it harder

> "Choosing one language over another feels like I am denying part of who I am. Is it normal to feel this way? How does a bilingual parent 'let go' of one of their languages when it comes time to raise their own kids?"
>
> Mariam Navaid Ottimofiore, *This Messy Mobile Life*

Olena Nesteruk and Loren Marks, professors at Brigham Young University in Utah, asked the parents of first-generation, highly educated Eastern European immigrant families living in the States how they defined their families back home and what effect does the distance have on their relationships. The scholars describe strong emotional Distance Familying as "an elusive goal". The immigrant parents regretted not having extended family around and not being part of a "big family". They try teaching the children their mother tongue, but most efforts still leave them disappointed.

When the grandchildren and grandparents don't share the same language

---

"When circumstances called into question the why and how of our family plan, we always remembered our family goal 'that our children will be able to speak

to both their grandmothers in their grandmother's language with no translator required."'
Josephine O'Brien, contributor to *Raising the Global Mindset*

French expat transition coach Melisa Cohen lives close to me as the crow flies - across a nearby harbour inlet. She has lived in Auckland for five years with her French husband and daughter. Her mother has visited but her father refuses to leave France, which makes keeping up connections that bit harder. Auckland is a melting pot of cultures, but you couldn't describe it as a city that embraces foreign languages. As a country, New Zealand teaches many languages in schools but rarely in a full immersion situation.

Melisa and her husband speak French to their daughter at home, but once the little one started at the local English-speaking school, their at-home French chat was never enough to maintain her fluency, let alone extend it. How could she communicate with her grandparents if she couldn't speak French? This became a big concern.

Melisa found a rare primary school offering three days a week full French immersion through an organisation called Frenz (frenzschool.org.nz). However, attendance would require a house move across town. It's tough to start again in another suburb when you're already new in a city, but they decided the move was worth it. A side benefit was the presence of other French families who, for the same reason, also migrated to this neighbourhood. It was all quite fortuitous that the assignment of Melisa's husband had them land where they did; in most other New Zealand cities, such educational facilities don't exist. What might have come of their daughter's competency in French and her relationship with her grandparents?

In another example, New Zealand grandparents Rhonda and Colin, who only speak English, have bilingual grown grandchildren in Germany. The three young adult German grandchildren have very different personalities, and each has embraced communicating in English with their grandparents at varying levels of enthusiasm. Rhonda and Colin admit to a little sadness that this has affected the closeness of their grandparent/grandchildren relationships. However, they're the first to say "kids are kids" and are very philosophical that you can't expect cookie-cutter grandchildren.

> "Miss 5 [daughter] advised this week that until my Danish sounds like hers and her dad's, then I shouldn't speak Danish."
>
> Keri (New Zealand Distance Daughter in Denmark)

Ideas for navigating grandparent/ grandchild language immersion

---

"Whatever language strategy you choose, make sure that your partner, your children's siblings, extended family, teachers, friends, etc., your village, is on board: you need a village to raise a multilingual child."

Dr Ute Limacher-Riebold cited in Mariam Navaid Ottimofiore's *This Messy Mobile Life*

Shannon Lanzerotta, another contributor to *Raising the Global Mindset*, quoted Nelson Mandela when he said, "If you talk to a man in a language he understands, that goes to his head. If you talk to him in his own language, that goes to his heart." Shannon emphasises that if Distance Sons and Daughters enrol their children in a language class, it's essential the children *like* their tutor. They must want to be around this person. "The relationship he [her son] began to develop with her [the tutor] became his motivation to learn her language."

Shannon has another little gem. She suggests hiring a babysitter or nanny who speaks another (different) language. You could, for example, target speakers of your parents'/grandparents' language. This would add another dynamic to your child's learning experience.

Distance Sons and Daughters, a practical suggestion I picked up from Ute Limacher-Riebold and Karin Martin is worth sharing with your distance parents. Once your children's understanding of their grandparents' language develops, let your parents know what's currently of interest to the grandchild, or what they are learning at school. Ute and Karin gave the example of water - as a science topic. The grandparents can then think of all the words in *their* language that relate to water (evaporation, humidity, temperature, liquid, and so on). Conversing in the grandparents' language, in this case about water, will help the grandchild improve their vocabulary. This shared experience can only do good.

Reflection

Language experiences within Distance Families can be so different. As a distance parent and grandparent sitting in New Zealand, I would rather cope with *all* our geographical boundaries (time zones, hemispheres, daylight saving and the International Date Line) than have any member of my family speak an unfamiliar language. We all have talents and I learnt a long time ago that mastering another language isn't one of mine. I am very grateful English is the primary language for all body parts (!) of all branches of our Distance Family.

10. NAVIGATING THE DISTANCE

"Family is something that we do, not something that simply is. More than this, the doing of family is never complete. It is always a 'work in progress'."
Neustaedter et al., *Connecting Families*

In this chapter I explore the practical day-to-day of *doing* Distance Families. I cover:

- Communication and technology
- Resources for your Distance Familying toolbox
- Gift-giving gems

You know how your family works. If you regularly find yourself on the same page as the folks back home, then pat yourself on the back. On the other hand, if you're sometimes frustrated and wondering if you could do things a tad better, this chapter is full of ideas you can dip into. Pick and choose what works for you.

Communication

Sociology professor Loretta Baldassar is a mobility scholar and Distance Daughter. She kindly wrote the foreword for *Being a Distance Grandparent*. In her research she talks about Distance Family communication. "What is often underestimated and unacknowledged about this kind of work is just how much skill and time is involved... as long as family members work hard at 'staying in touch' by making use of all the technologies available to them, they can maintain mutually supportive relationships across time and space."

Distance Family communication in all its forms can be hard work and requires commitment, effort, punctuality, sacrifices and being intentional.

Become a 'booker' and embrace the role of Communication Traffic Officer

---

"It is not distance that keeps people apart, but lack of communication."
Anonymous, cited in Ana McGinley's *Parental Guidance: Long Distance Care for Aging Parents*

I remember talking in South Africa with a local woman who complained she couldn't phone her New Zealand-based father whenever she felt like it. He'd chosen to leave his African homeland, and she saw it as her right to speak with him whenever she was inclined. I was already aware through other friends that well-functioning South African Distance Families are 'bookers'. In other words, they proactively create communication routines that all parties agree on. Knowing the family dynamics back in New Zealand, I gently suggested she become a 'booker'. She wasn't impressed.

One solution to Distance Family communication dilemmas is to embrace the role of Communication Traffic Officer and become a 'booker'. Imagine yourself standing in the centre of an intersection, fully conversant with time zone restrictions and deciding who can drive (or talk) and when. Distance Sons and Daughters may resent this responsibility, but the advantage is that much of the time you're in control, and that's a handy place to be. If family from afar experience an urge to ring you out of the blue at what might be an inconvenient time, they're less likely to do so if they know they're 'booked' to talk in a day or two.

Of course, chat routines don't have to be regimented. I'm also a fan of random potluck calls. In fairness, I receive them more than I make, but either way, each party knows that if the time isn't right, to speak up. I view random potluck calls as a bonus extra.

How to enrich existing communication routines

Small tweaks here and there can make a difference. Here are some ideas:

You cannot ring a two-year-old

This was the label of one of my key distance grandparenting communication research findings. Distance Sons and Daughters can feel bad when their children's availability is restricted due to naps and early bedtimes. Likewise, their parents/grandparents don't want to ring when it's not a good time. Most distance parents and grandparents rely on their children to initiate the bulk of the communication. Be a traffic officer; be a 'booker'.

Dr Kerry Byrne is a fellow crusader helping Distance Families. She shared a gem of wisdom: "Expect young grandchildren to engage for about one minute per year of life when you video chat. So if you get the four-year-old to chat or connect for four minutes, then pat yourself on the back." What a great guideline to work with.

Naturally, your parents and grandparents don't feel great when your children are asked if they'd like to talk with Nana or Grandad and they flatly refuse. Don't fret. Shrug your shoulders and accept that 'what is, is'. Everyone knows kids are kids, and it's the parents'/grandparents' responsibility to adjust their expectations and not get offended. Once again, perfection is not the goal.

Pretence: "we're fine"

There are many reasons why pretence exists between families. Do you hesitate to tell your Distance Family how you *really* are? In reverse, there's a difference between casually asking your parents "how are *you*?" compared with a deliberate and slow... "how *are* you?" Sometimes there are benefits in showing vulnerability.

Group calls versus one-on-one

Professor Emeritus Nancy Kalish is based at California State University. Her area of expertise is the rekindling of lost love. She made a statement in a *Psychology Today* article that *so* applies to Distance Families: "A preponderance of research on grandparenting confirms attachments are best formed by being with one grandchild at a time." It doesn't so much matter *who* they're talking to - it's the fact they have them *all to themselves.*

Regularly connecting with Distance Family as a group offers fun dynamics; group video calls are wonderful. But dedicated alone-time conversations are a gift and help upgrade communications from light and fluffy to a deeper connection.

Being on stage

Communication with Distance Family is dominated by video chat platforms, while in-country family communication is likely to be by text or in person. This means that Distance Families are continuously on stage - needing to perform. For some, this is a burden. There are people of *all* ages who honestly don't like video communication and would prefer they weren't constantly being seen on screen.

If you are among those who don't like being in front of a camera, your options may seem limited. If you speak up, it's likely you'll find that some family members are sympathetic, while others can't understand why you feel that way and could even be upset and see it as an affront. You could be opening a proverbial can of worms by speaking up. The solution instead is to be the initiator of other new mediums of communication. For example, text for no reason, or write a letter for no reason.

If you have family members who tend to be quiet during video calls, then *they* could be the uncomfortable ones. Once again, mix things up. Send them a text or letter for no reason and see what happens. If they are uncomfortable with video calls, you can be sure they'll respond with enthusiasm to other forms of communication.

The outcome of this strategy is that those who dislike video communication won't feel so obliged to be present during *every* future group video call: they have already chatted - albeit via a different method.

Quality versus quantity

Do you ring your parents briefly every day or have a jolly good catch-up once a fortnight? There are pros and cons to all routines. What works best for *you*? Do you know what your parents/grandparents *prefer*? There can be benefits in standing back and asking this question of yourself and them. What works when children are little, changes when they're at school and away from the house more. In *Chapter 21*, I explain how frequent communications (quantity) are preferable when your family is ageing.

Sharing the load

Some Distance Son and Daughter couples decide to take care of communicating with *their* side of the family, rather than always leaving it to the default 'organiser' in the household. This arrangement has its advantages as each set of parents/ grandparents is assured of talking with their direct family member. But that doesn't mean parents/grandparents don't enjoy hearing from their Distance Son-in-law or Daughter-in-law. Once again, there are no hard and fast rules: do what works.

Sometimes, one half of a couple makes more of an effort than the other to communicate with the folks back home. It doesn't take long for the distance parents of the less proactive one to figure out that their daughter-in-law or son-in-law is much better at this communication thing than their own son or daughter. My take on this is 'that's life'. Some accept this, some don't. But it's good to be aware, and as Distance Sons and Daughters, you can only do your best.

Time zone troubles

Time zones are non-negotiable factors in Distance Familying that make, break or at least muddy efforts to connect. On-the-move expats report how dynamics change when they move between assignments. Near and afar family members have to adjust to connecting at different times of the day. When our daughter lived in Bangkok, we'd hear from her during our afternoons or evenings. Now she's in America, it's our mornings or afternoons. At her end it's usually dinner time, so we tend to see our grandkids at the scratchy end of the day. There's little we can all do about this.

It saddens me when I hear Distance Sons and Daughters despair that their parents or grandparents regularly get time zone differences mixed up and ring at the wrong time, resulting in an interrupted night's sleep. This is unfair and uncaring.

There's no shortage of ways to figure out if *now* is a good time to phone. If this is *your* family, get creative on your laptop. Type up a chart showing times in both locations (summer and standard time) so your afar family can see at a glance what time it is at your place. Print and laminate it in different sizes (wallet size, iPad size and/or Post-it size for the computer monitor). Even glue on a magnet and make one a fridge adornment. If you think your family might get offended if it comes from *you*, have your kids design and gift wrap it instead and feature a show-stopper family photo. Better still, if your parents/grandparents don't take life too seriously, include two photos: one of you awake and one of you asleep.

The written word

I am a big fan of the written word. None of us write enough letters.

Older people remember when snail mail was an integral part of the tapestry of life. Never feel that writing a letter is a waste of your time. Even if you're telling them something you've already told them on a video call, it doesn't matter. My mother kept all the letters (and cassette tapes) I posted when I was a Distance Daughter. She passed them on to me years ago, and I confess they're stored away in a box of memorabilia in the attic space.

One of the loveliest stories I've come across was about a Distance Daughter who had a 21-year-old son. Celebrating a 21st birthday is a big deal back home in Australia. She posted a 21st card to all her son's old friends back home when it was *their* day. The young men were, as they say in Australia, 'stoked'. They couldn't believe she had gone to that much trouble, and they felt so special, even though they were far away. I remember feeling quite teary when she relayed the story.

Paddy Hartnett is my proofreader and lives in a small Norfolk village in the U.K. When insightful comments started appearing in my manuscript's comment section, I asked Paddy, "Are you a distance anything?" Paddy explained that he was once a Distance Son and recounted, "When I was 18 years old, I left home in London to go to university in Wales, and I stayed in Wales for 15 years. It was less than 200 miles away, but in those days it seemed much, much further. It was a big milestone. The day I left London, my father took me to the train station, and as I went to board my train, he stuffed a wad of cash in my pocket and started to cry. It was the only time I'd ever seen him cry, so I knew something big was happening, and then I started crying too! The reason I tell you this is that for the next three years, my mother wrote to me (snail mail) *every week*. Without fail. She'd just update me on the family gossip and check I was okay. I'd rip open the envelopes - I loved getting those letters. As I was reading your book, I realised that I never, not once, sent her a written reply. I'd ring her, of course, but I never sent a letter, and I regret that. As you say in your book, we don't write enough letters. I think writing to me helped Mum. I know she missed me, so it gave her a connection. And it gave me a connection too."

Dr Karen Eriksen is a friend in Sydney and for many years was a Distance Daughter. She is German, and her husband is Australian. When her parents were declining back home in Germany, it made her reflect. "A letter gives more time to digest and react suitably; a Skype conversation is instant and coarse. My mother couldn't really tell me on Skype how much worse my father's health was, as he could hear her, and I didn't want to worry her about my teenage son's depression - in the hope she wouldn't find out ever."

The ultimate in Distance Family written communication is a note from a grandchild to a grandparent. Ask each child to send a letter to their grandparents every couple of months, for no particular reason. To make this happen, a smart thing to do is have a communal place where note paper, blank cards, envelopes and stamps reside. Do a bulk shop - it makes it easy for everyone. You'll never throw out an unused stamp! The grandparents are sure to reply to these treasured one-on-one communications, and you can be certain every letter is cherished, read countless times and never thrown away. The absolute pinnacle is a thank-you note for a present.

In reverse, if you know your children would love to receive letters from your parents and grandparents, tell them. Not all parents and grandparents are blessed with the creative ideas gene, and they would welcome suggestions to enrich communication. If the grandparents and grandchildren speak different languages, this could be an exciting initiative.

I loved this idea from Rhoda, whose mother was unable to get out to the shops as easily:

> "I promised my mum I would get her some cards delivered. One of us [distance sisters] will pre-write addresses of grandkids on them. We will also give her the correct stamps. Then all she has to do is write on the cards and put them in the mailbox. I will also have gifts delivered to my sister (who now lives close by), and she can box them up and include birthday cards so Mum can send parcels for the grandkids."
>
> Rhoda Bangerter (Distance Daughter in Kyrgyzstan, mother in Wales)

Disconnected technically

In *Chapter 9* I spoke of the disconnect between generations who don't share the same language. In a way, technology is like another language. Some Distance Sons and Daughters may find it helpful to think of digital technology in this way when their parents or grandparents struggle. It's frustrating when parents/grandparents are reluctant to embrace technology: Distance Sons and Daughters know they're all missing out on so much.

Dr Stephen Golant is a professor at the University of Florida and a fellow of the Gerontological Society of America. He adds much wisdom to this discussion, and we will catch up with him in *Chapter 21*. In his research, Dr Golant explains that smart technology offers adults the promise of having more healthy, independent, comfortable and active lives.

Seniors' uptake of technology comes in many forms, including acquiring a motorised can opener for arthritic hands, a robot vacuum cleaner to eliminate a physically exhausting housekeeping task and, of course, owning (and using!) a mobile phone, iPad and/or computer. What surprises me is how older folk vary enormously when it comes to embracing technology. You can meet someone in their 90s who is technically connected on many levels, while someone in their 70s has nothing but a traditional landline.

Why is it that some people take up technology and some don't? Knowing the answer to that question may help reduce your angst.

Dr Golant explains there are four factors that influence whether older people will positively embrace smart technology options:

1. How **stressed** they are about their current situation. This creates a sense of urgency.
2. Their **perceived competence**, willingness and flexibility regarding new technology
3. How persuaded they are by **external information** (media, professionals, vendors, friends and family)
4. How persuaded they are by **internal information** (previous negative or positive technology experiences)

This offers Distance Sons and Daughters bad news and good news.

The bad news is that encouraging your parents and/or grandparents to embrace new technology is complicated. The decision may seem a 'no brainer' to you, but there are many reasons it might not sit right for your family member... just now. So never give up.

The good news is that you aren't the only influence in their lives. Other people are likely to be saying the same thing as you.

Let me share a story.

My mother lives in a lovely retirement village. When a new technology option becomes important to her, she researches and becomes an oracle on the subject. Both **external** and **internal** information influence her. One of the most critical sources is the information she gleans from her fellow residents. When one or two embrace a new product or service and they share this information, the research process is shortened.

One of her friends has just a landline telephone. Mum and other friends have encouraged her to "get with the times". They discovered she actually had an uncharged, disconnected mobile phone gathering dust in a drawer, along with a Wi-Fi connection she didn't realise she was paying for. Progress is slow, but this lady is now taking baby steps to use her mobile phone.

What's the moral of this story? Never give up on the digitally disconnected. You don't know who's muttering in their ear, trying to move them along.

Toolbox Reading

There are two books I highly recommend, even for the best functioning families. Neither author wrote with Distance Families in mind, but the principles are universal. When time, energy and opportunities are restricted, these books will help you 'distance family' *smarter*.

It's All About Relationships by Dr Karen L. Rancourt

When I read this book, I wondered how I'd ever got through life without losing every friend and family member. So much of Karen's wisdom can be applied to Distance Familying, particularly when relationships are maintained by a thin veneer of video calls and occasional visits.

Dr Rancourt differentiates between three types of relationships:

- **Secondary relationships** (Easy, casual friendships, connections or associations that come and go in our lives. These *can* include less immediate family.)
- Civil, cordial **'Have-to'** relationships with emotional distancing ("Because someone you do care about has enlisted you to do so, or simply because it is in your best interest.")
- **'Want to'** relationships ("Yes, I would like to get my needs met, but at the same time I would like you to get your needs met, too.")

Dr Rancourt gives you permission to categorise relationships, all the while conducting yourself in a congenial manner. In other words, it's okay to feel warm and loving towards your mother, and lukewarm, for whatever reason, towards your mother-in-law. There is a way to act and react to your mother and another way to act and react to your mother-in-law. What a gift.

The 5 Love Languages by Gary Chapman

An oldie, but a goodie. The book's key message is don't love people the way *you* like to be loved - show them love in the way *they* like to be loved.

There are five love languages, and one of them will resonate stronger for each of us.

1. Acts of Service (when people do things for you - you feel loved)
2. Gifts (when people send you letters, give you trinkets, buy you flowers, send you a card for no reason and never forget a birthday - you feel loved)
3. Quality Time (when people give you their undivided time - you feel loved)

4. Physical Touch (when people give you hugs, cuddles, handshakes and warm embraces - you feel loved)
5. Words of Affirmation (when people praise you and recognise your efforts and this boosts your feeling of well-being - you feel loved)

Once you understand the love language of each family member, especially those at a distance, you can make a few simple changes to the way you connect with them. This is working smart *and* with certainty.

So how do you do this at a distance?

Acts of Service

This love language is about *doing* things for others. It's as simple as being punctual and respectful of people's time. When it's someone's birthday, put up some balloons or signage as a backdrop to your video call. Offer ideas about how grandparents can connect with their grandchildren (topics to talk about, things they can do online). Make it easy for them. When your parents are elderly, you can phone them more often or take care of online grocery shopping. They're all distance Acts of Service.

I am an Acts of Service love language person. When I receive a gift that obviously took a lot of thought, the associated thinking process almost means more to me than the present. I would add *thinking* and *remembering* to the Acts of Service list.

Recently I was told of an elderly gentleman who was the greatest conversationalist and all-round loved guy. He had a card system to record conversations with people he met. When he saw them again, he was able to ask after them in a personalised way. When conversing with your parents/grandparents, make a note of what you could follow up on in the next chat. They will love it when you remember, and they don't have to bring the subject up in between all your news.

Gifts

Gifts love language people are easy to pick out. They hold on to every trinket, postcard, ornament, souvenir and grandchild painting. Their home can feel cluttered. The Gifts love language is not so difficult at a distance. Simply never forget a birthday, Mother's Day or any celebration when a card, not necessarily a present, is the order of the day. You can also embrace the likes of the balloons example in *Acts of Service* above.

Quality Time

Believe it or not this is one of the easiest love languages to deliver at a distance. It is so simple. When you communicate, put everything to one side (mobile phone, eating, driving, walking). Give the person your 100% attention. They would rather have a 15-minute quality conversation than an hour in the car while you're driving.

Physical Touch

This is the hardest at a distance; in fact, it is impossible other than blowing a kiss at the screen. But you can acknowledge your desire to give someone a big hug and keep repeating it. It is okay to say "I wish I could give you a hug" and to always add symbols for hugs and kisses in your messages.

Words of Affirmation

Once again, not so difficult from a distance. Always speak well of people. Leave messages they can re-listen to. The Marco Polo app works well for this. Build them up and encourage them, and be extra careful with negative reactions, harsh words or well-meaning advice. Words of Affirmation folk can dwell on these words forever.

Figuring out the love language of your Distance Family is not something you can do overnight, especially if you're new to the extended family. Keep Chapman's book handy, look for clues and when the right answer appears it will be obvious. As you figure out the love language of each person, your Distance Familying will become so much easier and smarter. Then you can confidently dispense with ways of loving that are almost a waste of time and focus on the best approach for each person.

You'll find additional recommendations in the Resources section at the end of this book and online at www.DistanceFamilies.com, where I keep a regularly updated Resources page.

Gift-Giving Gems

Gift-giving across the seas can be problematic. We all love receiving a parcel in the mail, but the cost of postage is sometimes hard to justify. During the COVID pandemic, entire countries decreed they weren't accepting mail destined for particular countries because of shipping and freight issues. Children outgrew clothes that had been purchased for them on the other side of the world.

Gift-giving routines evolve and change. For Clive and me, if our children are struggling financially, there's no joy for us have them spend money on us. Our family is flexible and easy-going in the present-giving department (in both directions), and we never get upset if presents aren't on the agenda. At the same time, I need to explain that the *Gifts love language* isn't predominant in our Distance Family, and this may well contribute to our casual attitude.

After U.K. Customs slapped our son with a whopping VAT bill for a Christmas parcel, we reverted to sending gift cards. But even these are troublesome as so many outlets only offer hard copy gift cards, not e-cards. Similarly, most U.S. online retail platforms insist that an American ZIP code is entered in the billing address field. 'Foreign' addresses have no home. No one from outside the U.S. can shop there. Thank goodness for Amazon, who are credit card user-friendly.

If you can get around these annoying issues, a little online creativity can produce some terrific gift ideas. We've given annual zoo, aquarium and theatre passes. Restaurant and garden centre vouchers are well received. Online wine orders are savoured, and manicures and massage vouchers are cherished treats. One word of warning, though: *Gifts love language* family members don't adjust easily to 'voucher only' and/or 'present-free' regimes. Sensitivity is required here. For *Gifts love language* family members, vouchers can represent a lack of effort - a 'make do' present.

Travel gadgets

Just a couple of left-field gift suggestions if parents/grandparents are planning a visit and Distance Sons or Daughters are stuck for ideas:

- Noise-cancelling headphones (the soft-padded type). These are the *best* thing to have on a long-haul flight. I can't recommend them enough.
- If visitors are transiting between long flights without access to an airport lounge, check if there's a non-airline-affiliated lounge you can somehow gift them access to. As we all know, walking into an airline lounge is like arriving at the gates of heaven.

Say it with flowers

I recently received some congratulatory flowers from an overseas friend. What a joy. Here they were, delivered with a press of the doorbell.

It reminded me of my youth when my advertising executive father managed the Interflora account. As a teenager, I thought Interflora was very glamorous. How amazing it would be to receive flowers from the other side of the world. This was well before the internet, a time when important messages, including flower orders, were sent by telegram. Like the written word, flowers have power. These days we can still use Interflora, or we can go online to any florist in the same suburb as our Distance Family and pay no more to have flowers delivered than if they lived down the road. Good to remember.

How you can win serious brownie points

After all my years of distance giving and my many chats with distance parents and grandparents, I can offer three hints in the gift-giving department that guarantee a HUGE R.O.I. (return on investment):

1. Send thank-you notes (in some form or other)
2. Don't forget Father's Day and Mother's Day - wherever you live
3. Be on time or early: work backwards

Send thank-you notes

Grandparents repeatedly tell me how disappointed they are when a gift isn't acknowledged (as mentioned earlier in *The written word* section). My English distance grandparents sent presents in the post when I was a child. My mother insisted we sit down and write thank-you notes. These first lessons in the art of letter writing taught me a lot. Even a simple email is better than nothing.

Mother's Day and Father's Day

Do you live in a country where Mother's Day and/or Father's Day lands on a different date from where your mother and/or father live? Do you curse when the appropriate greeting card isn't in the shops when you need it? This is a dilemma for Distance Sons and Daughters.

At the other end, it's a tough gig for the mother and/or father when *their* local day passes with little or no acknowledgement. The shops are full of merchandise, and Mother's Day or Father's Day is plastered across the radio and television. On the day itself, every café is full of families treating Mum or Dad. It's an unnecessary and painful reminder of the Distance Family void.

If your current regime is to send a card when it's *your* local Mother's or Father's Day, I'm sorry to say you've missed the boat. It's just not the same - but the folks back home will never tell you. This situation is easily solved, and the minuscule effort required to fix the problem will be rewarded with overflowing gratitude and appreciation.

So what's the solution? Buy a card (and even a spare) every time it's Mother's Day and/or Father's Day where you live. Put the cards aside and send them when it's the right time.

While I was writing this section, it was Father's Day in New Zealand. Every year I face the reality that our three distance adult children may or may not remember it's Father's Day in New Zealand because it lands on a different date from where they live. Yes, they should remember and put it in their calendar, but if I can't be sure, I take matters into my own hands and send them an email reminder. As a postscript to this, it would never occur to my husband to email my kids ahead of Mother's Day in New Zealand. But somehow, they always seem to remember. Kudos to them.

Be on time or early: work backwards

These days, you can't always rely on airfreight. Gone are the days when a letter travelled between continents in just a few days. Work backwards in your planning whenever you need to send a gift. For example, if you live in the U.K. and your father is in Australia, his Father's Day is the first weekend in September. To be on the safe side, you'll need to have his card in the post by the end of July - when some Northern Hemisphere-ites might be on their summer vacation. Smart Distance Familying takes some brain-frying planning.

Never worry about your post turning up early. It might be intercepted by the other parent and hidden away, and you can be assured that, on the day, they'll inform the recipient how early the card arrived. Or the envelope might be given a temporary home on the kitchen counter until the big day arrives. This kind of planning can become a badge of honour for Distance Sons or Daughters. It provides physical evidence of a desire to do the right thing and is a reminder of Distance Family love and devotion.

Reflection

This chapter has featured a myriad of ways to navigate the practical day-to-day of Distance Familying. I will finish with a family saying that has worked for us and perhaps might work for you.

"This is what our family does"

This is a line my husband and I have often used. On one occasion, when our children were still high-school-aged teenagers, we left them to fend for themselves while we travelled to the U.K. to visit my stepson and family. Rest assured, we left them a freezer full of meals. They also had their driver's licences and access to a car, my parents lived nearby and we had a couple of staff members who would come to our home office Monday to Friday. Before we left for the U.K. we sat the kids down and said: "This is what our family does, meaning that Dad and I need to visit the U.K. and we need you to co-operate, act responsibly and not be a worry to us." They understood and they kept their side of the deal.

You might decide that there are some absolute non-negotiables in how you navigate the distance between you and your family, whether it's regular video calls or your children taking on some of the communication responsibility. You too can proclaim: "This is what our family does."

Illustration by Cath Brew
drawntoastory.com

11. DISTANCE FAMILY RELATIONSHIPS: IN GENERAL

"Transnational family relations take a lot of hard work, involve much emotional labour, and represent a specific social reality that deserves attention."
Zlatko Skrbiš, *Transnational Families: Theorising Migration, Emotions and Belonging*

This is the first of five chapters about Distance Family relationships. The other four cover:

1. Parent and grandparent relationships
2. Siblings and other relationships
3. Upset and mayhem
4. The LGBTQ+ community

You won't find any hard and fast, 'must do', magical family action steps anywhere. There will, however, be a large dose of realism - and troublesome topics aren't brushed under the carpet.

Perfection should never be the goal. It is what it is. More than likely you just need reassurance that you're doing pretty well - right now, given the circumstances. From my observations most Distance Sons and Daughters, most of the time, are doing just that, and that's my overriding message.

Overall Strategies

First, here are some umbrella principles you might find helpful.

Forget happy-happy families

I have met dozens and dozens of Distance Families, and I can categorically confirm that not one of them is a 100% happy-happy clan. We're human, and whether we're living down the road or separated by thousands of miles, families are never perfect. And don't be fooled when those Facebook and Instagram photos give a different impression. There's always something going on behind the smiling faces.

Most of the families I have met are well-intentioned and doing their best. Most of the time they're succeeding and occasionally they're not. So completely disregard any notion that your family should be some kind of turbo-charged, happy-happy Distance Family. It's a fallacy.

What is your Distance Family 'currency'?

I once stumbled across a delightful book like no other: *The Read-Aloud Family* by Sarah Mackenzie. Sarah is a home schooler, which puts her in a saintly category that I have never aspired to join. She is also founder of the Read-Aloud Revival (www.readaloudrevival.com), which encourages reading aloud to children, and not just when they are young.

Her book introduces the concept of a family 'currency'. For her, stories are a family currency. "The words and stories we share become a part of our family identity... Kids whose parents believe reading is first and foremost a mode of entertainment and enjoyment end up being more voracious readers than those who want their kids to read so they can succeed in school."

In a similar way, Dr Charles Majuri, a child clinical psychologist and horticultural therapist, champions the nurturing benefits of shared intergenerational gardening activities. They generate:

- Trust - trusting what you plant will grow
- Sincerity - being honest and genuine individuals with your grandchildren
- Wisdom - decisions based on experience will bring success
- Patience - to endure without complaint and learning about delayed gratification

My best Distance Family success stories revolve around cooking, gardening and reading because I am reasonably good at them and they're of interest to my family. They are my Distance Family 'currencies'.

Finding your Distance Family currency is helpful. What interests do you have in common with your parents and/or parents-in-law and extended family? Is it fishing, art, football, running, board games, kite flying, camping or something else? These will always be the easiest to nurture. Stick with what you're good at and accept that some things aren't your cup of tea. Comparing your currency to that of other families is a gigantic waste of time.

Best not to live in a time capsule

It is easy for Distance Sons and Daughters reflecting about home to remain in a time capsule, unaware that just as *they* are getting on with their life, the same is true of their parents.

It's something I've experienced personally. Clive and I offered to host a live-stream wedding party when our Chicago-based son, Robbie, got married during the COVID-19 pandemic. Earlier, Robbie and Jen had sent a 'Save a Date' to the relatives and a bunch of his old friends at home in New Zealand. I needed to 'take over' that list as the starting point for our event.

I also mentioned to Robbie that we had friends *we* would like to invite. When some on that list were tenuous from his end as he couldn't recall them or he hadn't even met them, he was understandably concerned that our guests, unfamiliar to him, might outnumber his own old friends. I emailed back explaining the background of some of these people. Many were fellow distance parents and grandparents who we'd gravitated to over the years. We'd supported each other and knew all about each other's kids, even if we hadn't met them. They'd always 'been there' for us. Robbie's thinking hadn't allowed for our moving on and making our own lives. In the end, the old and the new shared a truly memorable time - laughing and crying together.

Truth and distance

"Honesty in relationships has its own set of rules and nuances, many of them shades of grey. Not grey is this fact: there is no such thing as 100% honesty in a relationship, including an ongoing and mutually engaging want-to relationship... White lies are like a social lubricant: they keep things running smoothly... lies and secrets can have a neutral, negative, or positive impact on a relationship."
Dr Karen L. Rancourt, *It's All About Relationships*

All generations of Distance Families struggle at times to tell the truth. As explained by mobility scholar Professor Baldassar, "Concern about how much information should be divulged, or is being divulged, is common as family members manage 'truth and distance'."

Distance Sons and Daughters naturally wonder if they should protect their family from bad news. Are they obliged to tell their Distance Family what's going on? As Baldassar tells us, when the answer to this question is murky, it leads to negotiated forms of coverup, hiding the truth, and suspicions. Family members begin to read between the lines, listen to the tone of voices and interpret silences.

Most distance parents and grandparents I've met prefer the truth. They're grown-ups. Sure, they may freak out at first, but they'd still rather know the truth.

> "My mother got COVID but didn't tell me at the time. I know she was trying to protect me, but I wish she had been upfront. Now there's a part of me always wondering whether she is telling me everything."
>
> Judit (Hungarian Distance Daughter married to an Italian, living in Hong Kong)

I am not saying Distance Sons and Daughters should pour their heart out if they are struggling to feel settled in their new location, or that they should divulge every less than favourable diagnosis from the doctor or every crack in the marriage. Absolutely not. But I *am* saying that open and frank conversations come with benefits. Your life is your life, and you have every right to keep your world private as you feel appropriate. But so has your Distance Family - and that may not always be to your liking. If you are open, then maybe the folks back home might be more open when you really want them to be. Follow your gut.

The Distance Family Thinking Pie: How Big Is Your Slice?

The Distance Family Thinking Pie is a symbolic reminder that each generation *thinks* about each other according to their own set of scales. The slices of thinking vary in size.

"The Distance Family Thinking Pie is a symbolic reminder that each generation thinks about each other according to their own set of scales. The slices of thinking vary in size."

Let's consider how The Distance Family Thinking Pie is divided between the generations.

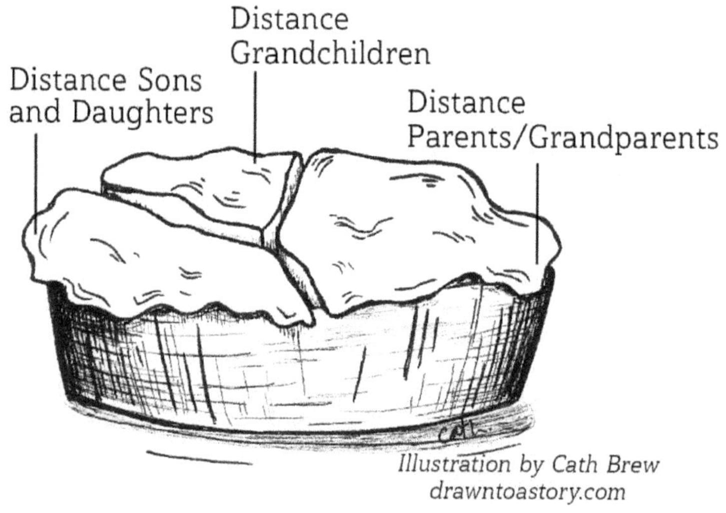

Illustration by Cath Brew drawntoastory.com

Distance parents and grandparents consume the biggest slice of The Distance Family Thinking Pie. They think about their distance (adult) children most, followed closely by thoughts of their distance grandchildren. They worry, they grieve, they feel the void: their Distance Family is constantly on their minds. When they wake up each morning one of their first thoughts will be, *are there any messages overnight from the kids?*

Distance Sons and Daughters think about their distance parents often, but not as frequently as their parents think about them in reverse. Theirs is a middle-size slice. Keeping with the same example, first thing in the morning, Distance Sons and Daughters have a full to-do list. They don't necessarily have time to ponder about their parents as they are rushing to get on with the day. There is only so much space, or 'bandwidth', as they would describe it.

The only time the size of the slice of The Distance Family Thinking Pie increases for the sons and daughters is when perhaps a parent is unwell and uncertainty about their future is a lingering concern. It is then the slice sizes of The Distance Family Thinking Pie are adjusted.

Distance grandchildren consume the smallest slice of The Distance Family Thinking Pie. Most distance grandchildren don't think about their distance grandparents much, but it doesn't mean they don't care. Most of us didn't think about our grandparents much at the same age. Their brain space focuses on many other things, and that's perfectly normal.

There are exceptions to the rule. I have come across grandchildren, more especially those who grew up geographically close to their grandparents and later moved away, who are very devoted to their distance grandparents. They are constantly thinking about them. However, they are the exception.

The purpose of talking about The Distance Family Thinking Pie is not to critique each generation's efforts. It is there for one purpose only: to highlight the reality that the quantity of Distance Family *thinking* varies between generations. This provides a context for realistic expectations of each other.

There is no right or wrong answer about how much thinking time to dedicate to your Distance Family. If the family is functioning well and everyone's needs are being met, as best they can be, that's an excellent result. However, if Distance Families are not functioning so well, it might be the portioning up of The Distance Family Thinking Pie isn't quite right. Reducing your expectations of the other generations will likely find you thinking less about what you have no control over.

Navigating Roles

Being single

Couples dominate this book's narrative. However, there is an enormous population of single Distance Sons and Daughters who navigate choppy foreign waters. Their situations vary:

- Never - or currently not - partnered/married, with one set of blood family members to connect with
- Separated/divorced, with their own family and the 'leftovers' of an in-law family
- Separated/divorced and co-parenting a child or children, with one set of related family members and the 'leftover' in-law family, including the other grandparents who will always be the grandparents
- A single parent by choice, with just their own extended family
- A single parent by choice, with their own extended family and 'other' side family as a result of adoption, fertility support or surrogacy
- Parenting alone because their partner/spouse is constantly away with their job
- A married/partnered couple geographically separated by choice or other circumstances

These scenarios are all very different, but if all of them were gathered in the same room, they'd have such a lot in common. Being single, or at least being by yourself geographically, adds both simplicity and complication to Distance Familying. For some, there's just one Distance Family to keep in contact with, but the buck stops with them for just about everything. There is no one to lean on.

Being a couple

Expat/migrant partnerships and marriages are tested to the max when living abroad. Distance Sons and Daughters don't have close family to leave the children with if they'd like a date night. They're very much on their own. That's fine when things are ticking along nicely, but when challenges crop up, Distance Sons and Daughters look with envy at their friends back home - who have their family handy.

In the early days of a relationship, discussion about what passport/s you hold and which country they entitle you to live and work in isn't always a hot topic. It's vital to discuss this type of red tape if you are contemplating expat/migrant life together or applying for entry permits, work visas, permanent residency or citizenship.

Distance Daughter Keri Bloomfield is a New Zealander living in Copenhagen with her Danish partner and a young New Zealand-born daughter. She is the author of the very amusing book *Nothing Like a Dane*. Keri explains that if you're a non-EU citizen like she is, and take on a Danish partner and have plans to live in Denmark, it's a case of 'buyer beware': "If you're on a Family Reunification Permit, you have to sign an Integrations Contract involving compulsory Danish language lessons and 'catch-up' meetings with your integration consultant whenever they request to see you." As Keri lamented, "Rather than immersing yourself in your new home according to your own timetable, there are milestones with deadlines you're expected to achieve." If all things linguistic are difficult for you, then this is a quiet and lonely burden. Few people, near or far, understand the pressure.

Australian author and Third Culture Kid consultant Tanya Crossman is married to an American. They spent the first two years of their marriage together in Beijing. When the COVID-19 pandemic locked Tanya out of China, they knew one would have to emigrate to the other's country. They chose to settle in the U.S., but immigration rules required Tanya to live outside the country while her Green Card application was processed, expected to take about 18 months. In the meantime, her husband had to begin life and work in the U.S. without her. With very few options, Tanya went back to Canberra to stay with her retired mum and dad. As a 30-something with dreams and goals, and as much as she loves her folks (and they love her), this wasn't part of the plan. For her parents, it wasn't quite the retirement they had imagined.

As I write, Tanya is still in Canberra. Having Tanya in town through all the pandemic lockdowns has been a godsend for her sisters, and she has loved the closeness she's developed with her nieces and nephews. One day she'll look back on this time and realise what a trooper she has been, but right now, all she wants is to be with her husband and enjoy normal married life.

When your partner is a local and you're an 'import'

If your spouse or partner is living in their home country and you're the migrant/expat, in many respects, the local has it easy because everything is familiar. The required adjustments are lopsided because the 'import's' burden is immense while they work at blending in. At times, this responsibility comes with a veneer of aloneness, something only fellow expats/migrants understand. Often, that aloneness is much worse than the 'other half' appreciates.

Border closures as a result of the COVID-19 pandemic didn't exactly help. When some governments proclaimed that expat nationals couldn't visit home, there was a sudden upsurge in Distance Sons and Daughters wanting to visit their home country. It was more than homesickness; these feelings came from somewhere much deeper. Too often I heard, "My partner has no idea how I'm feeling," and, "They don't understand my gut-wrenching need to visit home with the kids."

These scenarios shake the foundations of expat/migrant partnerships and test the resolve of being a Distance Son or Daughter.

Being a parent

Parenting when you are 'foreign' or you're in a foreign land differs from parenting when everything around you is familiar. The latter offers so many take-it-for-granted norms that are not available when you're new in town. As a result you do more together as a family unit and have to be there for each other in ways regular 'at home' families don't need to.

Parenting away from the traditions of home gives you the freedom to parent as you please without the influences and expectations from home. This was perfectly evidenced one evening when I was waiting at our local Indian restaurant. As I waited for my chicken biryani takeaway, I started chatting with a new dad. Asleep on his chest was a precious four-week-old baby, secure in a front pack. In a newly-arrived South African accent, he explained with conviction how skin to skin contact with his child was important to him. From what I've studied and witnessed of the patriarchal tendencies of a good proportion of the male Afrikaans population, this Distance Son was boldly demonstrating a contemporary parenting regime that I couldn't imagine seeing in Johannesburg, Durban or Pretoria.

Interestingly, when I shared this story with a friend and local scholar, Kris Finlayson, who is researching South African migrants in New Zealand, he added further layers to the story. He agreed with my observation on the surface but told me there were encouraging signs of intergenerational changes in South Africa. This leads me to believe the country is slowly catching up with the rest of the world. He added, and I found this quite an eye-opener: "Afrikaans men will do just about anything for their kids. The only people that cried during my interview sessions were men, and it was because they were in the early stages of migration and still wondered if they'd messed up their kids'/family's future." These are deeply personal sentiments from men who regularly deliver a heavy-duty presence.

As Distance Sons and Daughters, it is tempting to compare. Once again, this story confirms it's a waste of time. We never know what's happening for others when we meet them.

Babies

Distance Familying changes for everyone when babies arrive.

I have observed and followed many grandchildren born overseas and can report:

- If it's the first child for you and the first grandchild for your parents, the rites of passage are in disarray. The distance, void and emotions for everyone are at an all-time high because this precious new bundle means *so* much to *so* many.
- If it's not the first child/grandchild, it is tougher in practical terms for the Distance Son and Daughter but emotionally smoother for everyone. This precious bundle means just as much, but now everyone has adjusted a bit - good to know if you're contemplating a second or third.

Being a distance grandchild

When families move overseas, or children are born overseas, it doesn't take long before the middle generation realise their children have an altered identity from their own. Yes, the children's 'home' or passport country is a part of them (culture number one), but they are also part of the country they are currently living in (culture number two). These children are becoming global citizens: the world of globalisation and mobility is their *third* culture. They are Third Culture Kids (TCKs).

Illustration by Cath Brew
drawntoastory.com

Third Culture Kids, the enduring book by David C. Pollock, Ruth E. Van Reken and Michael V. Pollock, is onto its third edition. As the years have passed since the 1999 first edition written by Van Reken with Michael Pollock's late father, David, they have moved from historical discussions about expat children attending boarding schools in the home country, to the current global business of international schools situated just down the road.

Most distance parents and grandparents don't realise it is possible to own these multiple identities, but when the term Third Culture Kid is explained to them, it's like turning on a lightbulb. It brings clarity as to why these children are neither one nor the other. If you suspect your parents back home have little knowledge or even an appreciation of this concept, you might like to buy them a copy of *Third Culture Kids*.

If you're reading this as a distance grandparent, I recommend you become familiar with the terminology. Each day your grandchildren are living overseas, their identity is changing. They are becoming Third Culture Kids.

What this means - as it does for me - is that a distance grandchild isn't *all* South African or *all* Canadian or *all* Australian or whatever nationality the grandparents are. They have absorbed and embraced different customs and cultures and may not act and be like the other grandchildren (their cousins) at home. Some distance grandparents adjust better than others to having a globally diverse family. It can be confronting, foreign and challenging.

Distance grandchildren will feature in the third book of this series, *Being a Distance Grandchild*. The book's subjects will range in age from newborn to heading to retirement because it's a title you carry until the day your grandparents pass.

Being a friend

Quickly making friends in a new location is paramount to the success of settling and feeling secure. It isn't long before an authority, for example a school, asks Distance Sons and Daughters for a backup emergency contact - someone who's not your spouse or partner. That's tricky when you don't know anyone.

I have observed hardened expats who are used to being on the move become experts at making friends. They soon realise they need to go out on a limb, talk to strangers and introduce themselves in situations they might not do at home. There isn't time to take things slowly because tomorrow that person may head somewhere else.

Making friends as a new migrant in a regular suburb or neighbourhood, away from expat communities, is harder. Everyone you meet has established circles of friends. They are living a 'normal' life and they may not have a vacancy for someone new in their world. This can be a lonely place and it takes courage to start conversations at school gates, church services and sports activities.

Bridget Romanes is the founder of a relocation support company in New Zealand and warns her new arrivals about this likely scenario as it is regularly the case here. She encourages clients to have three sets of social connections:

1. Maintain connections with friends and family back home
2. 'New Zealand' local friends
3. 'International/expat' local friends

These three provide balance and when combined can offset, to a large degree, the day-to-day ups and downs.

Friends as family

Sociologists Raymond Pahl (1935-2011) and David Pevalin, both from Essex in the U.K., analysed data from a 10-year British household survey looking for patterns of family friendships versus non-family friendships. One of their findings was that family can feel like friends, and friends can feel like family.

As Distance Sons and Daughters develop friendships, some move to a level, over time, when they take on a surrogate role: surrogate grandparents, parents and siblings.

> "It takes a village to raise a child, and everywhere we have been, the girls have had aunties and grannies to care for them. They are no substitute for our family back home, but they do come a very close second. And when you don't have a choice, they are an essential support."
>
> Emily Rogers (Australian who has lived in India, China and New Zealand)

"I think part of what also happened because I moved around a lot as a kid and I didn't have a big extended family like you [Michelle] did, was my friendships became really important. All my buddies who you still know... all the guys I grew up with and have stayed in touch with all these years. That was my crew, that was my family."

President Barack Obama

I live in Auckland, one of the most culturally diverse cities in the world, with the fourth-highest foreign-born population. Amongst our friends are many Indian and Iraqi migrants. They work hard filling the family void they know the other is experiencing. I *can* be a friend, but I am not the same as someone from home.

I know my overseas adult children have friends who are like family to them. When you talk to your Distance Family about how special your new local friends have become, I would suggest there is wisdom in keeping your radar well-tuned. Your parents' every instinct tells them that your friends are a blessing, but there may be a part of them that is feeling demoted and redundant. Should that special local friend be a mother figure or a father figure, you need to be especially vigilant. Never apologise for this friendship. It is precious. But just know that some parents will embrace and celebrate it more easily than others.

In reverse, if your distance parents or grandparents visit, don't hesitate to 'share them around' with your local family-less friends. Your parents or grandparents will be sympathetic to your friend's plight and more than likely delight in 'being there' in whatever capacity they're useful. I've had conversations with Distance Daughters who have appreciated these extra bonus people popping into their lives for a cup of tea or a chat.

Reflection

The common thread here is that there are no hard and fast rules about *how* we *do* Distance Families, just as there are no hard and fast rules about how families 'family' at home. When challenged with a tricky situation, don't waste time with thoughts of failure: there's no 'pass' or 'fail'. As I said at the beginning, most families are doing their best, and that is as much as can be expected. What's important is to constantly remain open to the odd tweak here and there to enhance the good work you're doing.

Ronald Rolheiser, a theologian, teacher, author and lay priest, offers great wisdom here. In an article titled 'Faithful friendship', he writes about the family and friends we gather in life. As he reflects,

"How does one remain faithful to one's family, to old friends, former neighbours, former classmates, former students, former colleagues, and to old acquaintances?" Should we remember everyone's birthday and attend every family event, wedding or funeral? This, Rolheiser explains, would be a full-time job and is impossible. His advice is that being faithful to friends and family is not about how often you physically (or digitally) connect but about living within the "spirit" you once shared with that person. In other words, it's about having a relationship that when you *do* connect you seamlessly pick up from where you left off. No excuses are needed.

12. DISTANCE FAMILY RELATIONSHIPS: PARENTS AND GRANDPARENTS

"Throughout much of history, relations between the generations and with extended family members were conducted under rigid social rules about proper conduct. Nowadays, people struggle to reconcile different value systems regarding what family members ought to do for one another and feel at a loss for rules to guide their behavior."
Karl Pillemer, *Fault Lines*

"A majority of parents today are in far more contact with their adult children than were prior generations."
Joshua Coleman, *Rules of Estrangement*

The most important family relationships for Distance Sons and Daughters are with their parents and parents-in-law, and often they're the hardest. It's easy to think that how you and your parents operate is the same as everyone else, but that's not the case. Some adore their parents and parents-in-law and can't wait for the next visit, while others dread every connection. Some families talk daily and others once a month; for a few, it's hardly ever.

In a conversation I had with psychologist Karina Lagarrigue, she explained that the middle generation's personality traits, together with their upbringing, affect the ease with which they navigate living abroad. Her early PhD research findings on the topic indicate that the parents' ability to 'be there', even at a distance, decides whether Distance Sons and Daughters see them as 'role models' or search elsewhere for mentors. However, 'being there' doesn't come with a manual. Parents and parents-in-law can misdeliver.

The purpose of this chapter is to remove or reduce the grey areas between Distance Sons and Daughters and their folks back home.

The Past Matters

"Grandparents [and parents] may be aged anywhere from their late 30s to their 90s, and thus barely middle-aged, ageing or elderly. They are a diverse group whose values and experiences as grandparents will be shaped by the social history they have lived through, the quality of the relationships with their own children, and their level of participation in the workforce."
Deborah Dempsey and Jo Lindsay, *Families, Relationships and Intimate Life*

In his very helpful book *Rules of Estrangement*, Joshua Coleman explains that the rules of family life have changed over the past half-century and that, sometimes, either one or both sides can't or don't understand this.

In years gone by, *doing* families was pretty black and white, with little talk of emotions. These days there are many nuanced, grey areas that demand far more thought and reflection. As Coleman explains, "What [today's] younger generations consider harmful or neglectful parental acts would barely be on the radar for parents of almost any generation before... The belief that one should respect his or her elders has been replaced with the truism that respect isn't given, it's earned. Values, that once prioritized the family - these include obligation, responsibility, loyalty - have been radically reconfigured to emphasize the happiness and well-being of the individual."

Understanding Generations Matters

"Each generation develops a mindset and patterns that are unique to it."
Jim Burns, *Doing Life with Your Adult Children*

Nuances between generations can't be ignored. Below are the commonly quoted generational descriptions.

- Boomer 1/Silent Generation (born before 1955)
- Boomer 2 (born 1955-1964)
- Generation X (born 1965-1980)
- Generation Y/Millennials (born 1981-1995)
- Generation Z (born 1996-2009)
- Alpha Generation - sometimes now called Generation COVID (born 2010 onwards)

I'm not a great fan of these sorts of labels, but the facts can't be ignored. We are each a product, right now, of what we grew up with, which we thought was perfectly normal at the time. Being conscious of generational characteristics increases our understanding of the subtleties of each generation and how these could, in turn, affect Distance Familying.

Let me share some oddball examples from my upbringing.

First, my mother (Boomer 1/Silent Generation) would never sit in her father's armchair and neither would I (Boomer 2) sit in my father's armchair, even as an adult. It was a no-go territory - all about respect and honour and acknowledging the importance of the breadwinner's role. These days, we consider such talk patriarchal and demeaning to women, but for many, including me, it felt safe and appropriate *at the time*.

Similarly, babysitting by grandparents wasn't the done thing when I was a child to the degree it is today. My grandparents never babysat me. They either lived too far away, were unable to because of bad health, or passed away early. None of them saw it as a duty.

I mention these examples because traces of your parents' upbringing may rear their ugly head in ways you don't appreciate or welcome. If you understand *why* this happens, empathy becomes a helpful tool in your arsenal. Perhaps one day the environment and modes of generational thinking that *you* adhere to will become out of date and unwelcome.

An amusing postscript to my mention of armchairs is my aversion to a couple of pride-of-place, bells-and-whistles armchairs dominating a living room - in front of a television. When we moved into our current house and treated ourselves to some new furniture, I made sure it was sofas, sofas and sofas because to me they felt young and contemporary and armchairs felt old - and I didn't want old. I wonder where that thought came from?

Distance Family generations maintain relationships that are not only separated by oceans but also layered with historical social history.

Mothers and Daughters

In my research I discovered that female Distance Family members do more familying than their male counterparts. They say more, they think more, they have more opinions, they do more and they definitely experience more emotions. This is *not* a criticism of men. It's a fact.

Some mothers and grandmothers are a total joy, and some are a complete pain. Most have their moments and are a bit of both. Some distance mothers *obsess* about their role, others are middle of the road and a small percentage are a tad 'ho hum'. In *Rules of Estrangement*, Joshua Coleman talks of grieving mothers who make heartfelt cries and lament that life has no meaning without their children and grandchildren. This is a difficult extreme to live with.

Distance Daughters often say they appreciate and understand their mother better when they have a child. This is normal and bodes well for healthy relationships.

Mothers-in-law

"Every in-law problem is a marital problem if the couple aren't in agreement."
Carolyn Hax, *The Washington Post*

In *Being a Distance Grandparent* I discussed difficult Distance Daughters-in-law at length, and I promised "to set the record straight" in this book about the trouble-maker tendencies of some distance parents and grandparents. So here it is.

When I observe mothers-in-law who have two or three sons (in-country or overseas), I am fascinated by how differently each mother-in-law/daughter-in-law relationship pans out. The same woman can feel *so* welcome at one household and unwelcome at another. Is the daughter-in-law the troublesome party? Maybe, maybe not. A friend of mine who has married sons gives the following advice to future mothers of the groom: "Wear beige and say nothing." Most mothers-in-law I know, including me, are very aware of our precarious position and do our utmost not to upset.

Without a doubt, though, mothers-in-law from hell do exist and what's more they come in many flavours:

- The disapproving type, for whom nothing is good enough
- The "How dare you take my son" type
- The putting down the daughter-in-law type, who makes the latter feel like ****
- The "Everything is grander and better where we come from" type
- The "When are you going to give us a grandchild?" type
- The "Why did you take our grandchild away?" type

Some of these behaviours are downright mean, while others come from a place of ignorance, thoughtlessness, grief, anxiety or loss, or even as a result of mental health issues. The old saying 'hurting people hurt people' is never truer than with mothers-in-law from hell. However, for every dubious mother-in-law, there is one who *so* wants to be the best mother-in-law they can be.

Being a Distance Daughter-in-law

Being a Distance Daughter-in-law, just like being a distance mother-in-law, is fraught with dangers, booby traps and unknowns. Neither has had long to get to know the other. It's a package deal, whether you like it or not.

In *Being a Distance Grandparent* I wrote of 'gatekeepers' and 'gate openers'. In general terms, gatekeepers are Distance Sons or Daughters who for whatever reason discourage and/or restrict family communication. Gate openers intentionally encourage connections.

To be more exact, Distance Daughters-in-law fall into four categories:

1. Proactive gate openers
2. Reluctant gatekeepers
3. Deliberate gatekeepers
4. A confused and upset combination of all three!

I am a cheerleader for you all.

Proactive gate openers are the in-law's dream. In fairness, their job is probably made easier by having accommodating, accepting parents-in-law. This is a blessing for all.

Reluctant gatekeepers *want* to be proactive gate openers, but their mother-in-law is so troublesome (in reality, or it seems that way to them) that they are forced to impose some barriers and boundaries to make life bearable. Most of the mothers-in-law concerned are unaware they're doing wrong. The geographical distance is a blessing for these Daughters-in-law.

Deliberate gatekeepers may have issues regarding insecurity and need a sense of control. Their mother-in-law (and maybe everything about her partner's home/country/family) is a threat to her. Most of the Daughters-in-law in this category know they aren't being helpful. The geographical distance is a definite blessing for them. For the distance parents/grandparents, the geographical distance just adds to their woes.

Finally, there are well-meaning Daughters-in-law who from time to time **experience all scenarios** in a mixed-up, confusing, trying-to-please-everyone mess. Included here are Daughters-in-law who speak a different language from their parents-in-law and those who are divorced and perhaps coping with co-parenting situations. *Everything* about being a Distance Daughter-in-law is hard.

The point of defining these scenarios is to do two things:

1. Highlight how different these relationships can be

2. Assure you that others are in the same boat: yours is not a unique experience

A contributor to *The New Granny's Survival Guide* (published by Gransnet in the U.K.) had this to say: "I think the old saying 'A son is a son till he finds him a wife, a daughter's a daughter for the rest of your life' is so true. My mother-in-law was very nice when we were 'courting', but as soon as we announced our engagement she went on the defensive. It took us until my son was born to get over our differences and we became the best of friends. I miss her so much since she has passed away; all I can say to all mothers-in-law and daughters-in-law is: learn to live with each other as individuals, and not enemies fighting for the son's attention. You might find your best friend." *glassortwo*

I would describe the daughter-in-law/mother-in-law relationship as a constant 'work in progress'. This book will offer you small, incremental suggestions to help you navigate the space. When you reach the stage where both of you can be frank and open and caring and loving - all at the same time - you'll both breathe a sigh of relief. And so will everyone else.

Distance Daughters-in-law who seriously struggle with their role will find ways to categorise and compartmentalise their relationship in *Chapter 14*. It may help switch off the pressure.

Piggy in the Middle - Please Take Charge

> "My sister-in-law back home has disinvited my recently widowed mother for Christmas. My brother hasn't stood up to her. He hasn't turned around and said, 'no'. She coaches her kids and says, "It's Mummy's turn to decide where we have Christmas this year and who gets to join us."
>
> Anonymous Distance Daughter

This topic is aimed at Distance Sons. I will be frank with you. Time and time again, when niggly conflict surfaces between a Distance Daughter-in-law and her in-laws (not necessarily just the mother-in-law, maybe the whole in-law family), Distance Sons are nowhere to be seen. Often, distance parents might not even know there's a problem, or if they do, they can't understand what's wrong and why. This can all lead to ghastly estrangements and unnecessarily cutting off access between grandchildren and grandparents.

Distance Sons, what is coming from your parents is nothing new; it's been the norm, all your life. By now you've probably grown accustomed to their way of seeing things. When you don't agree, you more than likely prefer not to rock the boat, and when you're sympathetic to their point of view, it may well be because of your longitudinal gaze.

Separately, you can see your partner's concerns too. You will want to sympathise there - your relationship with your partner is number one, and she desperately wants you to back her up and be her hero.

What often happens, though, is... a big fat nothing.

"When your parents apply their pressure on your life decisions, you make it clear you intend to decide for yourselves."
Carolyn Hax, *The Washington Post*

As someone who can see both sides of the story, you can smooth waters by speaking up. To put it bluntly, take on the difficult job of dealing with the issues, *in a timely fashion*. Complaining about being 'piggy in the middle' isn't helpful. Do what needs to be done. Everyone will benefit - including you.

Fathers and Grandfathers

When conducting my formal university research, I decided that interviews with *couple* distance grandparents would happen with both halves present - in their home. With a cup of tea in one hand and a scone in the other, husbands opened up, and that might surprise some Distance Sons and Daughters. Even though 'the men' can appear a little aloof about all things family, as a bunch, they're well and truly in the Distance Familying trenches. They tend to take a step back and allow their wives to be centre stage because they know how much the grandmother role means. Never see this as a sign of disinterest. Given the right setting they have lots to say and are just as keen as their wife to pore over photos and videos that land overnight on their mobile phone.

The other role they perform *so* well is the smoother of troubled waters. If there are Distance Family problems, they offer a lending ear and a less emotional voice of reason. When a baby is due or there is a crisis on the other side of the world and Distance Sons or Daughters yell "help", they are also the ones tolerating an empty house and lonely mealtimes when their wife jets off. Sometimes they're still working to pay for the airfare.

I salute distance fathers, fathers-in-law and grandfathers.

Encourage Parents and In-laws to Mix - If It's Feasible

A framed cross-stitch of delicate pink and mauve sweet peas hangs in our sitting room. The English mother-in-law of my stepson crafted it. We have known her for around 25 years, and every time we visit, she invites us for coffee at her local village Costa. Like many of the grandparents of this generation who have lived through World War II, she isn't prone to displays of emotion. On our last visit, my husband and I were taken aback when she slipped us this handcrafted gift with her normal no-fuss demeanour.

The cross-stitch speaks volumes. We sensed a quiet acknowledgement that when our kids married, we got the 'distance deal' and she and her late husband got the 'close deal'. We'd also earned our stripes doing the miles to keep connections up. While I was writing this book, she became frail and died. We'll never have another coffee together at Costa. Our lives have been richer for her presence in our Distance Family world.

Distance parents and parents-in-law might be as different as chalk and cheese but what they have in common are their grandchildren and a desire for the family to be happy. We have always enjoyed catching up with the in-laws of our children, and I would encourage readers to do the same if it is at all possible. It's a win-win for everyone.

Unsolicited Interference, Advice and Questions

Family members who interfere, especially parents (distance or otherwise), are a problem. They may criticise life choices or how their grandchildren are raised. Most of the time, they don't mean to meddle but find themselves saying, "I can't help myself." Most distance parents and grandparents I've met know that to interfere and offer advice when it's not asked for is a recipe for family disaster. But that doesn't always stop them doing it.

Some distance parents never stop asking the question, "When are you coming home?" Understandably, this rattles the cage of the middle generation. Just because the folks back home believe their home location might be the best place to live, doesn't mean their son or daughter will automatically feel the same way. As the meaning of home sways and wavers, after a while there isn't an answer to the question. Distance Sons and Daughters change, but their parents aren't adjusting in tandem. This is troublesome but unsurprising.

I love this line from Lori Gottlieb, a psychotherapist and contributing writer in *The Atlantic*: "The job of an adult child [like a Distance Son or Daughter] isn't to manage a parent's worry, nor is it the job of a parent to manage that child's choices." Many readers will say Amen to that.

Later, in chapters about ageing parents, I will highlight that distance parents and grandparents aren't craving unsolicited advice or unwelcome questions from their Distance Sons or Daughters either. There are two sides to this discussion.

In the meantime, what is the solution to meddlesome distance parents and grandparents? I have two suggestions:

1. **Filter advice**

   As expat coach Victoria Tanner explains, "Remember that as much as you miss them, your family don't have all the answers. They have *their* answers to your problems." Some advice may apply and some perhaps not. Distance can infuse advice with a degree of weightiness that is a burden to deal with. It's harder to filter and shake off.

   Victoria advises surrounding yourself with people whose opinions and advice you respect. I would add that the context needs to align. You can respect someone's advice, but if the context isn't the same as yours, then you have to sift and sort to stay grounded.

2. **Learn from The Child Whisperer**

Carol Tuttle is the author of *The Child Whisperer*. In one of her podcasts, she shares the following about unsolicited advice. It's the best I've found anywhere:

- First, talk to your partner so you're both on the same page about whatever the issue is.
- Decide the No.1 thing you want to change. Narrow things down rather than having a long list.
- Decide how you are (both) going to tackle this issue.
- Work out what 'you don't want' and what 'you do want'.
- If you are clear about this single issue, it's likely the other problems will solve themselves.
- When you relay your concerns, say something like, "We really appreciate your support and your love for our kids, but we *don't* like... and we *do* want..."

  You can be pretty certain that if you follow Carol's advice, later that day when your parents are lying in bed together, one will say to the other, hopefully in a charitable way, "I told you so!"

  I loved a comment from a new mum and Distance Daughter who was coping with a visiting mother telling her how to look after the baby. She eloquently responded, "I take care of my baby. You take care of your baby [me]."

What Do Your Parents and Grandparents Want to Hear from You?

In *Being a Distance Grandparent* I explain to the grandparents that their Distance Sons and Daughters want to hear them regularly verbalise how proud they are of them and all they've achieved.

Distance Daughter Rhoda Bangerter read one of my early drafts, and one of her responses was: "What do *parents and grandparents* want to hear [from their distance adult children]?" That's an excellent question, so here are some suggestions.

- "I love you and miss you." (They are tough and can hack it.)
- "I understand this is hard/inconvenient/unfair for you, but I appreciate your support."
- "I would like to spend some time with just you."
- "I know the kids aren't great at communicating. Thanks for your patience - maybe next time."
- "Here are some online kid present ideas to make shopping easier."
- "When you come (or we come), what are a few things you really want to tick off?"
- "When you come (or we come), please speak up if we're too rowdy or you've had enough. I know you're not used to little ones, and I want you to speak up."
- "I won't be late."
- "I'm paying for this."

Reflection

Intergenerational distance parental relationships are so worth nurturing, and sometimes simply tolerating. When relationships are tested, take a deep breath and think of the bigger picture, not just *your* feelings at the time. There are no prizes for the best parent/in-law/grandparent relationship; however, you can be justifiably proud if most of the time your family functions in a zone where "we all get along pretty well". That, my friend, is a job well done.

13. DISTANCE FAMILY RELATIONSHIPS: SIBLINGS AND OTHERS

"A family is not simply a bunch of individuals who act independently, but instead is a system in which change in one person or relationship profoundly affects the others... For many people, simply knowing that one's siblings are present in the world and available in time of need is a comforting thought."
Karl Pillemer, *Fault Lines*

In this chapter, siblings, aunts, uncles, nieces, nephews, cousins, steps/blended and halves all get a mention. They represent the next layer of family afar. Time and distance affects these relationships. On the one hand, the physical distance makes life simpler and less cluttered, but on the other, there is a feeling of missing out.

Siblings

It never fails to amaze me how often two sets of genes produce offspring who are vastly different in personality and outlook. Families where all the siblings get along and thoroughly enjoy each other's company *are* the exception. Most are a motley bunch of good intentions, mixed-up emotions and vague respect. It's not uncommon to hear the familiar saying 'you can choose your friends but you can't choose your family'. Add geographical distance and perceived/actual obligations to your parents and the like, and being a distance sibling can be a fertile ground for all manner of emotions and mental gymnastics.

Just as there can be a distance parent/grandparent void, it can be the same, over time, with siblings. Each day they live apart, both parties realise they're getting on with their lives but not necessarily in tandem. It is a loss, and like all the other losses, can generate grief for what could have been.

"And don't even ask about the time I lived in Turkey [as a Distance Son]. I was extremely close to my youngest brother, who had a learning disability and lived with my parents in London. The geographical distance between us was very difficult for me, so I'd spend a fortune getting flights back to London to see him. Being a distance sibling was a nightmare."

Paddy Hartnett (Distance Son)

"My brother (in the U.S.) has divorced twice. Because we haven't been there on a daily basis, it is difficult to know what is really going on. My brother and sisters-in-law were trying to 'get us on their side'. I stuck with my brother. A few years later, my brother broke up with a girl he had been seeing for a year or two. It hit him hard. I stayed up and spoke to him at 2 am my time. He cried that someone would care enough to do that. He was alone, he had no nearby family to speak to. He thought we were all asleep because it was night-time in Europe."

Anonymous distance sister, Europe

"I have a younger sister. When I moved abroad my sister swept in and took up space for both of us. She had family before me so my mother became the grandma she wanted to be. It really helped to ease some of my guilt of being far away."

Melissa Parks (previously a Distance Daughter in Spain with family in the U.S.)

Melissa is now repatriated and is living near her family again. In a reflective moment, she admitted it would be pretty interesting to talk more with her sister about how those years were for *her* back then.

When distance parents die, local friends of Distance Sons and Daughters sympathise for a while, but in time, there's an expectation they will 'move on' and that the loss won't dominate conversations. Siblings are invaluable as they offer comfort well past society's accepted grieving timeline. They have a precious shared history.

In contrast, geographical distance can be a blessing for strained sibling relationships. It is not bad to feel this way, but never close the door to rekindling or improving bonds. There is more about this in the next chapter.

Aunts, Uncles, Nieces and Nephews

Aunts and uncles have a unique ability to fill voids. There's something about the fact they have the same genes as a parent. If there is parental disconnect, aunts and uncles become an important lifeline to home. They can also be another voice if Distance Sons and Daughters are concerned about ageing parents, and a comforting voice if a parent has passed. Most of the time their door is open, even if they haven't heard from you in a long time.

Distance Sons and Daughters who don't have children often take an extra special interest in nieces and nephews back home. These children love their exotic aunt or uncle and follow their every move with great interest. The nieces and nephews may even talk of wanting to follow in the footsteps of their aunt or uncle. Be aware of the example you are setting.

> "Video chats are amazing but they don't take the place of cuddling a niece or nephew, of interacting with them in person. I am so thankful for sisters who work to make sure I'm a part of their children's lives, but I still miss being able to see them in real life."
>
> Tanya Crossman (Distance Daughter)

Cousins

If a Distance Son or Daughter grew up with cousins nearby, it might bother them that their children don't experience the same connection. But it pays to remember that 'they don't know what they don't know'. For much of my childhood I had no cousins nearby, and I didn't realise I was missing out on anything.

Cousin digital meetups are a perfect solution, and most kids are very capable of making that happen themselves. It just takes one of them to kick it off. A bunch of adult nieces and nephews on my husband's side have regular Zoom meetups. They're spread around the world, and it's lovely to hear in passing that they're keeping connections up.

In *This Messy Mobile Life*, Mariam Navaid Ottimofiore cautions Distance Sons and Daughters against talking too much about their children's exotic adventures: it may appear like boasting or bragging to the family back home. Sadly, the children may need to tone things down when they talk about their own world. There is wisdom in reminding children that the art of good conversation includes asking questions first.

Steps/Blended, Halves and the Like

My research and personal experiences have confirmed that most remarried distance parents and grandparents are proactive when it comes to treating their combined families evenly. They try not to differentiate between steps/blended and halves, even at a distance. It's all about showing love and 'being there'. But for sure, there are exceptions.

Even if a distance stepmother or stepfather isn't on the Top of the Pops list, Distance Sons and Daughters will be pleased they're around if their mother or father on the other side of the world is poorly. Some stepfathers and stepmothers walk a precarious tightrope, and a cheerleader from afar means a lot.

In the opposite direction, if Distance Sons and Daughters have acquired new siblings (steps or halves) because a parent has remarried and are part of a new blended family, they might not be biting at the heel to be buddy-buddy with their newly gained family. As a stepmother of 30+ years and a stepgrandmother of 22+ years, I am here to say, "That's okay." When Distance Sons or Daughters connect as best they can, this is a generous act of love for their parent and step-parent. These seniors live with the knowledge that *they* are responsible for their mish-mashed, mixed-up family.

How to Keep Up Connections with Extended Family

Keeping up connections with extended family can appear overwhelming, but it doesn't need to be. Come up with just one or two things you do, remembering that consistency is important. Here's a few suggestions:

- Create separate WhatsApp groups for your parents/parents-in-law to ensure the dynamics are different.
- Initiate a once in a while video catch-up, ensuring time zones are well catered for.
- Tell them: "You're always welcome if you travel this way."
- Arrange an easy gathering when you visit home. For example, a bring-your-own picnic.
- Encourage your children to connect with their cousins (if they're open to that).
- Send an annual newsletter at Christmas, even if they don't do the same in reverse.
- Remember birthdays even if they don't remember yours or your children's.

The key to navigating extended family is once again to do your best while not expecting miracles. If you're always going the extra mile without comparing what you're receiving back, that's a good place to be.

Reflection

Warm relationships with distance siblings, aunts, uncles and cousins are there for the taking. They're the icing on the cake. What a bonus it is to wake up to an email from an extended family member who has taken the time and energy to connect.

14. DISTANCE FAMILY RELATIONSHIPS: UPSET AND MAYHEM

"When people don't drive us crazy, it usually means we're getting what we need from them (or we just don't care). So, when people drive us crazy, that usually means we want something from them that we aren't getting."
Carolyn Hax, *The Washington Post*

"There's an adage that goes like this: If you don't like someone, you should get to know them better. In other words, when you give someone a warm reception and approach them with genuine interest, you often find something likable about them."
Lori Gottlieb, *The Atlantic*

We each deal with family stress in different ways. My default regime is to take it all on board emotionally. The anthropologist comes out in me. I know how *I* think about the problem, but I want to understand the *why* and *how it is* for the 'other'. Why do they think that way? I envy people who can flush away family upset. I've come to accept that's not me.

This chapter is full of 'how to' strategies for trickier family situations. My game plan is to share the best advice I have come across - advice that can be effective even when geographical boundaries are thrown into the equation, though some creativity may be required. Even if your family relationships tick along nicely, you may well pick up some useful tips here.

I loved a comment from Dr Karen Rancourt in *It's All About Relationships* when she reflected on the terms 'conflict' versus 'discord'. In the first draft of her book, she used the word family *conflict*, but after discussion with her advance readers, she reverted to family *discord*. As they all agreed, conflict can elicit powerful emotions, while discord doesn't seem to do the same. If you have family conflict, consider renaming it 'discord'.

As you reflect on troublesome Distance Family relationships, keep in mind Dr Rancourt's advice from *Chapter 10* about how best to categorise a relationship:

- **Secondary relationships** (Easy, casual friendships, connections or associations that come and go in our lives. These *can* include less immediate family.)
- Civil, cordial **'Have-to'** relationships with emotional distancing ("Because someone you do care about has enlisted you to do so, or simply because it is in your best interest.")
- **'Want to'** relationships ("Yes, I would like to get my needs met, but at the same time I would like you to get your needs met, too.")

Reading Helps

"When interpersonal crisis is muddied with angry accusations, rigid expectations, defensiveness, and an inability to be sensitively aware of the other person's feelings, the likelihood is that everyone in the situation will lose. That is, the 'sparring' players will retreat to neutral corners, but each will

feel a victim - misunderstood, hurt, resentful."
Selma Wassermann, *The Long Distance Grandmother*

If you're living with seriously fraught family relationships, reading the words of experts definitely helps. The written word gives you three things:

1. Comfort - because you realise you're not going crazy and you're not alone
2. Clarity - because the authors make sense of what makes little sense to you
3. A Track - to repair relationships, should you choose to take it

What I am saying is that you'll feel better once you've read about your problem. A commitment to understanding why you think one way and why your distance parents/grandparents, for example, think another way will give you clarity.

The daughter of a friend has a mother-in-law from hell. When my friend poured her heart out to me about the family upset, I mentioned I had books on my shelf that might help. She borrowed some, including the titles below, and was over the moon when they helped her make more sense of their troubles. The books were passed on to her daughter and partner, who were open to any creative ways of addressing their problems. They even had a family meeting to discuss one of the books - it was that helpful - and went on to purchase their own copies. The mother-in-law won't change, but they have changed how they deal with her.

There are two books I particularly recommend:

1. *Rules of Estrangement: Why Adult Children Cut Ties & How to Heal the Conflict* by Joshua Coleman
2. *Fault Lines: Fractured Families and How to Mend Them* by Karl Pillemer

For further titles, please refer to the *Resources* at the back of this book and a regularly updated Resources page at www.distancefamilies.com/resources.html.

Circles of Concern and Circles of Control and/or Influence - Understanding the Difference

Emily Rogers is Australian and an expat family coach and founder of Expat Parenting Abroad. She is currently based in New Zealand. One of her very simple but poignant gems of wisdom is to remind yourself what sits in your Circle of Concern and what sits in your Circle of Control and/or Influence. It's about drawing a line between what you can fix (or make better) and what you can't fix.

When she spoke about her cancer-suffering dad back home, Emily was naturally overflowing with *concern* about a disease she had no *control* over. She FaceTimed her folks every day, even if her dad didn't always want to chat. She could *control* her calendar to work within the time zone difference and ensure the calls always happened. Her parents knew she was thinking of them every day. Emily also rang her mum each time Dad went to the hospital for chemotherapy. Due to pandemic restrictions, he went on his own. Emily could *influence* the outcome of her mum's day by 'being there' on the phone when her mother couldn't accompany her husband and had no one else to turn to.

It is perfectly normal to be upset about what you can't fix. Hanging around there, though, drains your creative thinking and makes you less effective at *influencing* things or making them better.

When Emily's father died, my heart went out to her. She promptly followed her own advice. Trans-Tasman borders were closed due to the COVID pandemic, so she couldn't fly to the funeral. Although very *concerned* for her mother, Emily couldn't *control* her inability to be there in person, but she could *influence* the outcome of the Zoom funeral. She bravely attended the live-streamed event with her family, and her mum sensed her presence. I have great respect for Emily's emotional resilience.

When I Hear the Word 'Toxic'...

"Being able to feel safe with other people is probably the single most important aspect of mental health; safe connections are fundamental to meaningful and satisfying lives."
Bessel van der Kolk, *The Body Keeps the Score*

"My daughter-in-law is toxic."

"My mother-in-law is toxic."

"My sister is toxic."

I am wary of declarations like this. I've witnessed situations where I've had good reason to believe the statements were false. I once heard identical cries from two conflicting parties in the same family, and because I knew the family members well, I was sure one party was right and the other was wrong.

I urge caution.

There *are* toxic family members, but rarely are two present in the same conversation. More often than not, one party will describe another family member as toxic when they aren't getting what they want. Then, when unreasonable demands are placed upon the second person, they label the attacker as toxic.

Writer Carolyn Hax has a wonderful advice column in *The Washington Post*. She has addressed this topic and suggests there is always a story behind the story: "It's like seeing the shadow of an object that itself is out of our view."

My interpretation is that there is a controller and a controlee.

> **"There is a controller and a controlee."**

One is leading the charge with destructive and unhelpful behaviour, oblivious to the fallout. The other is incredibly hurt, chasing their tail in disbelief and unable to make sense of anything that's said or done.

Imposing barriers and boundaries

A Distance Daughter-in-law will impose barriers and boundaries if she is critiqued and criticised by her mother-in-law (distance or otherwise). The daughter feels inadequate because the relationship, as van der Kolk explained earlier, is not safe. The senior is a toxic intrusion.

In reverse, when these barriers and boundaries are imposed on the distance mother-in-law, she views her Distance Daughter-in-law as toxic. The mother-in-law is usually at fault and is often blind to her behaviour.

There is another scenario. If a Distance Daughter-in-law has low self-esteem and/or feels threatened by her in-laws, she may worry that her partner will decide to move the family back to his home country - her worst-case scenario. Her defence mechanisms cause toxic behaviour, and her insecurities cause her to believe her in-laws are toxic.

Hax sums up controlling behaviour in another post: "When I notice myself tensing up and scripting my words in an effort not to touch off emotional consequences with someone, that's my aha moment that I'm involved with someone controlling. The people I trust, who are honest, who have sound emotional regulation, who accept me as I am instead of trying to change me, are the ones who don't erupt at things I say, even the stupid or inflammatory things."

In her award-winning book *Belonging: Remembering Ourselves Home*, Toko-pa Turner has some brilliant advice about replacing the need to control with vulnerability. As Turner points out, many of us can relate to feeling vulnerable and perhaps see it as a negative trait. And so she invented the term 'vulnerabravery'. "Instead of putting up our defences and demanding control when we meet with conflict, *vulnerabravery* is the conscious choice to keep our hearts open so that we might discover what's hidden within it."

Attachment theory

"The biologically based process of attachment persists and influences our emotions for as long as we live."
Karl Pillemer, *Fault Lines*

In a 2018 article, Professor R. Chris Fraley explains that John Bowlby (1907-1990), a British psychoanalyst, developed the theory of attachment when observing infants who would cry, cling and frantically search for a missing parent. Bowlby observed that children who grew up in insecure situations suffered as adults. Their relationships were dominated by insecurities, anxiety and avoidance.

It's trickier to apply attachment theory to geographically distanced adult relationships because there are already so many barriers and boundaries in the way. I am raising it now because if you have a troublesome relationship with the folks back home, it may clarify things a little. If a Distance Son or Daughter dreads communication and visits with their parents or in-laws in either direction, *and* anxiety and avoidance are constant companions, then maybe he or she has some mild, or possibly stronger, attachment issues.

Perhaps the physical distance is just what the doctor ordered as far as they're concerned.

As psychologist Joshua Coleman says, "I have worked with many families who had close, confiding relationships with their adult child but found their relationship completely upended by the children's new spouse. This was especially true if the new husband or wife was psychologically troubled. In those situations, the spouse feels threatened by the attachment of the adult child to his or her parents and eventually says, 'Choose them or me, you can't have both.'"

In an article for *Quartz*, writer Youyou Zhou outlined four attachment theory behavioural patterns found in close adult relationships:

1. Secure (low anxiety, low avoidance). These people enjoy a good level of healthy relationships.
2. Anxious-preoccupied (high anxiety, low avoidance). These people tend to worry a lot and need constant reassurance they are loved. They can be overly dependent on their partners.
3. Dismissing-avoidant (low anxiety, high avoidance). These people tend to hide their emotions and avoid intimacy.
4. Fearful-avoidant (high anxiety, high avoidance). These people desire closeness yet tend to keep their feelings to themselves.

There are two other factors to consider. First, a person may not exhibit the same attachment pattern to every close relationship. They may feel secure with some and insecure with others. Second, attachment theory and styles work in either direction. A distance parent or parent-in-law may, for example, display troublesome symptoms towards a Distance Son or Daughter.

If you are coping with a difficult family relationship, increasing your understanding of Borderline Personality Disorder may also help. As explained by Hans R. Agrawal and colleagues in a psychiatry review, "There is a strong association between BPD and insecure attachment... individuals demonstrate a longing for intimacy and - at the same time - concern about dependency and rejection." A useful book on the topic with an apt title is *Stop Walking on Eggshells: Taking Your Life Back When Someone You Care About Has Borderline Personality Disorder* by Paul T. Mason and Randi Kreger.

Bullying

Bullying is a close cousin of toxic behaviour. If bullying is present in your Distance Family, you are likely to be very grateful for the geographical divide. Distance doesn't solve it, but it can put it at arm's length, and that's a blessing.

Dr Keith Barry is an associate professor of communication studies at the University of South Florida and past co-chair of America's National Communication Association's Anti-Bullying Task Force. Professor Tony E. Adams is from Bradley University in Illinois and has a strong research focus on family communication. In a joint article titled 'Family Bullies', they argue three key points:

1. Family relationships are *voluntary* rather than involuntary, and estrangement can be an appropriate response to unhealthy family situations.
2. The context of bullying within a family differs from bullying with friends and can't be compared.
3. To understand bullying requires what scholars call an auto-ethnographic research approach. You need the sufferer to tell it 'how it is'. Surveys and questionnaires can never match the heartfelt words of someone who knows how it feels to be bullied.

So what does this all mean for you?

- You might need to reconsider how you view and connect with your troublesome family (think back to Dr Karen Rancourt's advice about categorising relationships).
- You can't compare family strife to friendship strife.
- Only you know how it is for you.

You can battle alone or you can battle with some cheerleaders. Dive into some books.

No Relationship At All

To those Distance Sons and Daughters estranged from their parents and/or grandparents, I offer you two contrasting comments from Joshua Coleman:

"Most parenting occurs in a fog where seemingly good decisions can later appear clueless, selfish, or damaging - and the parent deserves a chance to repair."

"I don't think adult children are obligated to have a relationship with a parent, especially in those cases where there's a history of abuse... To consider reconciling, an adult child needs to feel assured that they can return to the estrangement if they decide that reconciliation was a bad idea."

I love Coleman's frankness.

Therapists: A Word of Caution

Online and in-person therapists, counsellors and life coaches are common in expat circles. Distance Sons and Daughters have to cope with a lot, and having a listening, guiding ear can be an asset. However, I took notice when I read this from Joshua Coleman:

"It's not unusual for [parental] estrangements to begin

as a result of the adult child entering psychotherapy."
Joshua Coleman, *Rules of Estrangement*

This is a powerful statement and Coleman goes on to say: "Many parents are completely unprepared for the reflection of their parenting seen through the eyes of their [adult] child's therapist."

There is much that can be done before breaking ties. Reading the books I've mentioned is one course of action. You don't have to follow the writers' advice or even agree with their recommendations, but if you feel there is any chance of keeping a relationship alive, you'll be better equipped.

There are therapists and therapists. I would gingerly suggest that if you are experiencing what you consider are toxic connections from afar and the *first* advice from your therapist is to break ties - pause. Think of it like medical advice. Get a second opinion.

Political Polarisation

"Winning is not about asserting your position, it's about strengthening a connection."
Dr Tania Israel, *Beyond Your Bubble*

In November 2016 I was in Chicago when Donald Trump was elected president. I witnessed tears, emotions and despair within families. The day after the election, I was caught up in spontaneous street protests when Democrats let off steam. America taught me much about itself on that visit.

Political divides within the family are real and destructive, whether it's Brexit, abortion law, climate change, anti-vaxxers, gun laws or the U.S. Democrat/Republican divide. Communicating and interacting with your Distance Family when political divides exist is yet another barrier to overcome, or at least navigate.

Tania Israel holds a doctorate in counselling psychology and is a professor at the University of California. She has written a practical book titled *Beyond Your Bubble: How to Connect Across the Political Divide, Skills and Strategies for Conversations That Work*. One of Israel's reflections stands out to me as it offers a unique perspective: "People on each side [of any discussion] tend to overestimate these three disparities: the gap between the two sides, the gap between their own personal views and what they think the views of the other side are, and the gap between the people who are on what they perceive to be their side and people who they perceive to be on the other side of things." In other words, nothing is exactly as it appears.

Extreme views tend to dominate the media, and those responsible for these opinions are positive everyone thinks the same, while in actual fact, most people fall into what Israel calls the 'Exhausted Majority'. These people do have views, but they disengage or maintain a low-key stance because of the conflictual tone of the extremes. I relate this to an iceberg. What you see above the water are the most aggressive voices hogging the media. Under the water is a vast population that does have views, and may even appear pretty committed, but they quietly appreciate that there are other sides to the argument.

With the right techniques, most feuding and politically charged family members *can* find common ground *and* an improved respect for each other. As Israel adds, "Understanding people in the context of their morality, rather than our own, can help us to be more respectful of others' motivations, and respect is a key ingredient of successful dialogue."

Separation/Divorce

When my children were a toddler and a baby, my first husband left me for greener pastures. Solo motherhood wasn't much fun, but I picked myself up and worked through the stages of grief, determined to move on. A year down the track, when my ex announced that he and his newly gained family were moving overseas - on our wedding anniversary - to live in a suburb called *Helensvale*, I thought the day deserved some sort of odd recognition. Our older accountant friend, Clive, a divorcee and solo dad, had previously offered to take me out if I felt I needed company. As there were no better offers - in fact, *no* other offers - I asked if we could have dinner together that night. It was only supposed to be dinner, but here we are, 30-plus years married.

In recent years, I watched from afar as both my Distance Daughter and my Distance Stepson went through a divorce. I won't repeat their stories here, but if you'd like to know 'how it was' from the distance parent's perspective, grab some tissues and a copy of *Being a Distance Grandparent*.

Separation and divorce away from home is messy and scary. Jeff Devens, in *A Parent's Guide to Raising Kids Overseas*, confirms that there are no official expat/migrant statistics on separation and divorce, but he has seen figures as high as 60%. Devens also claims that "a significant cost for international families centers on the spouse who spends frequent periods of time away".

Every country has its own laws, and divorce can be taboo in some nations. Overnight, a partner can become homeless or stateless as a result of their 'accompanying spouse' visa being no longer valid. And if one or other of the separating couple continuously relocates with their job, how on earth do they navigate co-parenting?

Financial affairs may favour one spouse over another. When our daughter ended up divorced in the U.S. after living there for only two years, her limited credit history - including a small credit card limit - made it difficult to get loans and additional liquidity when she needed it the most. Her divorce also moved the goalposts on her eligibility for citizenship, which had a significant impact on her career trajectory inside the U.S. federal government agency she was working for. Depending on the circumstances, being 'stuck' in another country as a result of divorce and co-parenting custody arrangements can constitute a significant hardship.

Divorce and separation also affect members of the extended family, especially the parents and parents-in-law. New routines have grandchildren moving between two households, so opportunities to connect are reduced. Likewise, visiting parents/grandparents have reduced access to their grandchildren. Our daughter is fortunate to still feel very at home where she lives, but to have the possibility taken away from you of ever moving back to your home country or living close to family while your children are still under 18 is a loss - for her, the children and us.

I readily admit that a positive by-product of co-parenting is that distance parents/grandparents end up with more one-on-one communication time with their distance adult children. Most, like me, enjoy the luxury.

Reflection

"Kindness is freely at our disposal and can be used as soon as right now."
Inder Singh, founder and CEO of Kinsa

I have endeavoured to present this chapter without judgement while providing food for thought. But what's my opinion?

I offer two things:

1. Rarely, and only as an absolute last resort, estrangement has to be. Sometimes it is unavoidable. As columnist Carolyn Hax reminds us, estrangement is a choice that has to be made every day and renewed every day after that. Keep in mind the example you are setting for your children on the 'how to do relationships' front. Do whatever you can to teach them how to 'do families' well.
2. For the rest of your extended family, it's about two words: respect and kindness. None of us has to love and adore every family member, but we can decide which relationships are non-negotiable, if for no other reason than someone you love wants you to maintain that relationship - as outlined by Dr Rancourt. Your mother-in-law might not be your favourite person, but it's still possible to show a degree of respect and kindness because she means something to your partner.

15. BEING A DISTANCE CHILD (OF)

"Gender expansive and/or LGBTQ+ people have distinct stress as they move through the world navigating identities that are often misunderstood and marginalized... Being seen, safe, and supported for ***who you are****, and* ***whom you love****, are deep enduring gifts that heal hearts and keep families connected, even from afar."*

Dr Laura Anderson, child psychologist

Cath Brew is a red-headed Australian expat living in the U.K. and can be found at https://drawntoastory.com. By trade she is an artist and book designer, just two of her talents. Her gifted sketch artistry features in this book series. Cath is a night owl and often I would find myself 'talking' by email to her during my mornings and her night times, when I was sorely tempted to put my mother's hat on and say, "Go to bed - it can wait until tomorrow."

Cath also happens to be an advocate for all things LGBTQ+. When I asked Cath to define LGBTQ+ this was her response:

"LGBTQ+ is the acronym used to describe people's sexual orientation and gender identity who are not heterosexual and/ or cis-gendered (identify with their birth gender). It stands for Lesbian, Gay, Bisexual, Transgender, Queer or Questioning, and other sexual and gender identities."

In one of Cath's nocturnal communications, she challenged me and asked if I had considered calling this book *Being a Distance Child (of)*. She pointed out that this title would be more inclusive of the LGBTQ+ community: "I know many people who wouldn't refer to themselves as a son or daughter, as that falls into the binary of male and female. For example, my wife is gender neutral/queer and I've checked with them. Ang says that they would not refer to themselves as being a mother's daughter, but rather their mother's child."

As I had my breakfast and then took a shower, I knew that Cath's words had rattled my cage. I am the sort of person who thinks hard and fast when a tricky situation presents itself and the solution isn't necessarily obvious. I don't like to leave things hanging, even if my initial response is only a tentative one. I respected and appreciated Cath's comments, and an early acknowledgement was in order.

I replied to Cath and explained there were many reasons the title should remain 'as is', but I was hearing her point loud and clear, and it was important to me. I quoted a saying my late dad would utter. For many years he managed an advertising agency, and a saying he repeated to us kids was: "Don't hide it, make a feature of it." Over the decades I have applied this lesson. Rather than brush over something, I would bring it to the forefront. This chapter is me following my dad's advice.

I always intended to feature LGBTQ+ expats/migrants in this book, but out of Cath's exchange came an apt chapter title: *Being a Distance Child (of)*. I also gained a writing running mate willing to critique my privileged, heterosexual, white female, Baby Boomer perspective. I am good at putting myself in other people's shoes, but on this occasion, two heads are better than one.

Let's unpack LGBTQ+ Distance Children (of).

LGBTQ+ Distance Children (of) can be/are:

- Single expats/migrants
- In a couple relationship
- In a throuple or triad relationship (a committed romantic relationship between three people)

- Wives/partners
- Husbands/partners
- Parent as a single
- Parent as a couple
- Partners/Daughters-in-law
- Partners/Sons-in-law
- Siblings, cousins, godchildren and godparents
- Members of a new 'chosen family' who support them emotionally like a parent/parents

LGBTQ+ distance adult children share all the same Distance Familying highs and lows featured in this book, but for some, there is another layer of unwelcome life challenges placed unwittingly, and often silently, upon them.

The choice of country of residence has a huge bearing on the 'how it is' being a Distance LGBTQ+ expat or migrant. Many countries and cultures are LGBTQ+ friendly, and some are not. Quite simply, life for LGBTQ+ people is vastly different depending on where they settle.

An InterNations article suggests that when an LGBTQ+ expat/ migrant lives in a location that is less than LGBTQ+ friendly, the following may be experienced:

- A need for constant discretion about their private lives (to protect themselves). This includes giving an impression that couples are 'room-mates'.
- Problems applying for spousal visas
- Hefty fines for any form of non-traditional sexual relationship 'propaganda'
- Hostility, imprisonment and/or deportation

I asked Cath, "How is it being a Distance Child (of)?" and she explained that while the InterNations summary is correct, there is so much more to it because 'propaganda' can be as simple as holding hands in public or booking a double room. And while hostility, imprisonment and deportation are appalling things to experience, in some countries, the death penalty is a genuine possibility.

Cath went on to say, "My experiences as a lesbian have been positive, especially in terms of my family. I went to write 'I've been lucky with my experiences' but stopped myself. It saddens me I naturally go to write 'lucky' to describe being treated as I would expect any 'child (of)' to be loved and accepted for who they are. But for many this is not the case, and for all of us, being an LGBTQ+ expat or migrant brings to the surface, daily, extra things we need to navigate that our heterosexual friends do not.

"Even in the best circumstances when your family accepts you as an LGBTQ+ child, additional strains can arise for parent/child relationships if you live in a country that is not so accepting. As the LGBTQ+ child you may know how to keep safe, but your parents may not be as aware. As such, when parents visit the LGBTQ+ child abroad, the child may be more anxious and hyper vigilant to ensure their parent doesn't accidentally 'out' them and put them in danger. This can create tensions, especially if parents unwittingly feel that the hyper vigilance is unnecessary.

"For the LGBTQ+ child (of) and family, obtaining visas and entering countries requires extra preparation and care. I know of same-sex couples whose visa status as a family is less stable than it could be. Those with children can find one parent is named as the 'parent' on a visa (the birth parent), while the other parent only has access to a tourist visa for the duration of their stay. Tourist visas generally last 90 days - not long in the context of a 3-year expat post. Not only does this have implications for staying in the country long term, but also in emergencies and for your rights as a parent.

"If holidaying to a country where you're not too sure about how homosexuality is viewed, it is not uncommon to approach the immigration desk separately, as individuals, rather than as a couple. This is harder when you are a family. Does one parent (the birth parent) go first with your children and you go second and hope that you too will be let in? Sometimes when travelling abroad, I've even gone as far as removing pictures of me and my wife from my phone and have replaced them with a picture of me with a male friend on the main screen. It's always better to be safe than sorry or consider not visiting at all.

"Equally, all of these issues may be irrelevant when you're abroad but can be triggered when visiting family at 'home', especially if your relationship is not recognised in your birth country. When I got married, because same-sex marriage was not legal in Australia, my wedding was in my adopted country, the U.K. This placed a huge financial burden on family and friends to make the trip to the U.K. I was very fortunate that so many friends and family came over. However, had I been in a heterosexual relationship, I would have been able to enjoy an Australian wedding that local people could have attended more easily. And it's not just practical things like visas. Difficult emotions also arise. As my wedding was so far away, my grandmother could not travel, and it still saddens me she did not see me get married. To this day, I have still not had an Australian wedding.

"For some LGBTQ+ people, going 'home' to see family can be an extremely painful and anxious time. If a person lives an openly 'out' life in their country but is not out to their family, this can be incredibly difficult on a number of levels. Firstly, hiding who you are is emotionally draining; it not only takes a lot of work to maintain, but it can be isolating, damage your health and deny the core of who you are. In these circumstances going home is not desirable for the 'child (of)' and potentially creates strain in parental/child relationships.

"For the expat/migrant family with LGBTQ+ children, staying with grandparents can also be strained. I know of families where the grandparents want to see their children when they come home, but outwardly express their dislike of having an LGBTQ+ grandchild. This adds pressure and worries for parents as it creates stressful internal negotiations about the expectation of 'having' to stay with family or whether they are bold enough to choose a hotel. In choosing a hotel, it is important for parents to reaffirm to their child that the 'problem' is with the grandparent, not them. This can be a difficult emotional space for the grandchild and requires parents to be alert to the potential worries and thoughts that their child might be experiencing.

"Furthermore, visiting home when you're not 'out' and knowing how unsafe it could be if they found out is a terrifying prospect. This occurs especially when religious and cultural beliefs are at odds with LGBTQ+ people. At one end of the scale, time with family may be unsettling and uncomfortable, while at the other end of the spectrum, 'unsafe' may include verbal and emotional abuse, physical abuse and in some cases being killed in the manner of an 'honour killing'. Going home to visit family is never simple or safe in these situations. Choosing to live at a distance may be a conscious choice for the LGBTQ+ child, to keep themselves physically and emotionally safe. However, in doing so, sibling relationships, which are often more accepting, also become geographically distant, making connections to family harder.

"I also know of transgender grandparents who are not welcome in their child's house or to see their grandchildren. Any visits to see their children and to try to improve relationships require shortened visits or additional financial resources to afford hotel stays.

"There are of course many LGBTQ+ people who are open with their families but their sexuality and/or gender expansiveness is just being 'tolerated'. No LGBTQ+ person wants to be 'tolerated'. I have heard many say that it feels worse than being hated, because it is not overt. It's in the subtle comments. On the surface everything looks good, but the 'tolerance' becomes like gaslighting and plays unhelpfully with your mind. You might be married in the country in which you live, but when visiting family you're given the twin room or separate rooms because your relationship is not recognised by your parents. When introduced to your parents' friends, your partner is always introduced as your 'friend'. 'Uncle Dave' at the long-awaited family get-together makes a homophobic joke and none of your family call it out. Grandma continues to ask you when you'll find a nice girl to marry, despite you telling her repeatedly that you're a gay man. The frequency of these micro aggressions may accumulate to create a major impact. Frustrations, anger, mistrust and a whole lot of other uncomfortable emotions can arise for the LGBTQ+ child. Trips 'home' can be fraught with mistruths, discomfort and denial. Who wants that for a holiday?

"Similarly, when parents come to stay, some people feel unable to be themselves in their own home. I know of LGBTQ+ couples who, for the duration, sleep in separate rooms so that the parents continue to believe that the couple are platonic house mates. This hidden life also means that partners are not included in Christmas cards, are not sent birthday cards or are excluded from family gatherings - including weddings and funerals. There is coupledom privately, but publicly, you are single. In some relationships, only personal mobile numbers are used with family, so that there is no unwanted curiosity about who answered the house phone."

Being an LGBTQ+ ally

Being an LGBTQ+ ally is an important visible action for positive change. Here are some simple ways to make a difference to the lives of LGBTQ+ people:

- Listen and hear what LGBTQ+ people tell you about their experiences.

- Educate yourself and stay informed - follow LGBTQ+ people and organisations on social media and read reputable reports like the ILGA World's State-Sponsored Homophobia report.
- Do not 'out' someone without their permission.
- Never assume someone's gender or sexuality.
- Challenge homophobia, lesphobia, biphobia and transphobia.
- Examine your biases and prejudices. For example, if you wouldn't ask a heterosexual and/or cis-gendered person a certain question, do not ask an LGBTQ+ person either.
- In your marketing materials, include LGBTQ+ people and same-sex families.
- Use your pronouns (she/her/hers, he/him/his, she/they, etc.) on social media profiles, emails and public communications.
- Donate to organisations that support LGBTQ+ rights internationally.
- IGLA World - International Lesbian, Gay, Bisexual, Trans and Intersex Association
- OutRight Action International
- Rainbow Railroad
- www.stonewall.org.uk

Please be aware that being a visible LGBTQ+ ally in some countries may be unsafe. Act according to the laws of the country in which you are located.

Reflection

I am very grateful to have Cath for her contribution. She offers an insight that despite the best of intentions is hard for many of us to grasp in its fullness. As I ponder on this subject, a few things come to mind. One is a rant, for which I make no apology, the second is a thought about locations and the third is kudos for a job well done.

1. **Gender-reveal parties**

   As a card-carrying Baby Boomer, I just don't 'get' the contemporary trend of baby gender-reveal parties. This new rite of passage seems to go completely against the tide of gender inclusivity. In fairness, and with no concrete evidence to back up my claim, gender reveal parties don't seem to be particularly evident in globally mobile Distance Son or Distance Daughter circles, which is refreshing.

2. **Choosing a nation**

   When any potential expat chooses a new location to live, there are many reasons why one may look more appealing than others. It could be as simple as the weather, or proximity to the ocean, or career prospects. They're all valid reasons. For LGBTQ+ expats, knowing which countries are LGBTQ+ friendly and which are not is an important consideration. Do your research via trusted organisations and check the latest information via multiple platforms.

3. **Courage**

   It takes courage and tenacity to stand up for who you are and what you believe in - whether it is to your family, a future employer or an immigration department. Being a Distance Child (of) can be difficult.

16. VISITS: IN GENERAL

"The increasing number of people leading differently constituted mobile lives, and the spatial dispersion of families across multiple geographical locations, raises questions of how they maintain, and reconstruct, their family life and friendships."

Dr Hania Janta and professors Scott Cohen and Alan Williams, *Population, Space and Place*

For some Distance Sons and Daughters, visits are difficult affairs and they can't wait for normality to return. Others feel short-changed when it's time for one or other to leave. But for a third group, the visits are just right: their sense of family closeness is topped up and all parties are accepting of the global family dynamics.

Decision Making and Planning of Visits Is Often One-sided

My research and observations suggest that Distance Sons and Daughters make most of the decisions about what is happening where and when during visits (in either direction). In practical terms, when your parents travel to you, they can be very much in your hands, especially if there are language issues - so it's unsurprising you take control. And when you visit home, you know exactly who you want to see and what you want to do.

Parents' input varies. Some will drop a few hints about possible plans and hope they've been heard; others will be more upfront with their suggestions and make a definite request. But by and large, distance parents/grandparents rather *expect* to be organised or to be told what is happening. All of this isn't necessarily a bad thing. Most times, parents will willingly co-operate.

"All or Nothing"

Dr Sonia Jaeger is a psychologist and psychotherapist and the co-founder of Location Independent Therapists. Every day she supports expat and migrant singles, couples and businesses. When I discussed this book with Sonia, she mentioned what she calls the "All or nothing" factor. As she explained, whether a family visits her clients or they visit family back home, they all spend so much time together - perhaps too much time - that this can be a problem. Her clients don't get to experience the shorter, shared-everyday connections that happen when family live close.

Are there solutions? Well, yes and no. This is another one of those times when 'it is what it is'. I expand on 'All or nothing' in the next two chapters.

The Dichotomy of Babysitting

The prospect of parents/grandparents being handy to babysit can be the best news for some and the worst nightmare for others. Having parents and grandparents mind your children during visits, in either direction, can come with a litany of bewildering expectations and concerns, flip-flopping and confusing emotions from both sides.

What might we all be thinking?

Possible Distance Son or Daughter thoughts:

- "Thank goodness. The cavalry's here. I'm so looking forward to having some time out."
- "I'm so pleased for Mum and Dad. They naturally miss the kids and deserve time alone with them. I'll make it as special as I can when we visit."
- "My siblings at home get so much babysitting support. Now it's *my* turn."
- "Will they insist on looking after the kids their way and ignore our 'rules'? I'm a bit nervous."
- "I hope they don't come with a suitcase of sugary sweets."
- "Not having my parents handy has been a strain on our marriage as we've had so little time to ourselves. But I can't tell them that - it was my choice."
- "Can they manage? Are they too old to look after little ones now? Their house isn't kiddie-friendly."
- "They'll want to mind the kids, but I don't trust them."

Possible distance parent/grandparent thoughts:

- "I can't wait to spend every single minute with my grandkids. Nothing is too much trouble. I'm so excited."
- "I want to help out here and there, but it's been a while and I'm not sure how I'll manage with the kids."
- "Will the grandchildren like me?"
- "Last time they visited, all I seemed to do was housework and look after kids. I hope they don't expect the same thing this visit. It would be nice to do some fun things."

- "I don't think babysitting is part of a grandparent's brief. I'm not flying all that way to babysit."

I've heard *all* of these thoughts and I'm sure you could add more.

TulsaKids, an online family magazine, published a moving letter from a grandmother to her late mother:

> "Dear Mom,
>
> I wish you were alive so I could tell you how sorry I am. When I had young children, I was completely unrealistic in my expectations of you. I didn't understand why you weren't eager to step up and help me with my adorable babies. OK, they were precious, but now I know they were also a lot. Even at the time, I knew that two babies, just 15 months apart, were a handful. That's precisely why I was so desperate for help. I didn't understand that you didn't have the energy to care for little ones. I know you loved all your grandchildren, but you also had your limits... Now, I am the 63-year-old grandmother with two precious grandchildren I adore. I want to step up to the plate and be everything for them. My mind and heart are willing, but my body is not always in agreement. I have so much love for them, but as much as I hate to admit it to anyone (including myself), I have my limits... Please forgive me, Mom, and thank you for being the mother and grandmother you were!"
>
> Diane Morrow-Kondos

The message here is not to assume your parents and grandparents are built-in housekeepers and 'on demand' babysitters, even when they say "I'm fine". They are unlikely to tell you how they feel because it is instinctive for them to want to 'be there' for you. Insist on finding a happy ground where they can 'do' for you, you feel supported and there's also some downtime for everyone.

The solution to all of this is communication. It's a good idea to reach out to your parents/grandparents before visits occur and chat about these issues. They might not know for sure about childminding duties until you've arrived or they've landed and recovered from jet lag, but even *that* is good to know. You want to know where you stand, and they want to know you've thought about their needs and that you care.

Here's one approach to try: "Mum/Dad, we want you to enjoy your stay and spend time with the kids. But we don't want to impose and have you take on more than you want to. So please speak up now and during your visit. It's really important to me/us."

Who Pays for What During Visits?

Who pays for expenses during visits, in either direction, can be tricky. There are many factors at play. But for sure no one wants to sit at home for every meal. We all want to get out and visit places together.

Should expenses be the exclusive responsibility of the highest earner or the one with the greatest discretionary income? Distance grandparents may know, for example, that the family of their son or daughter is struggling financially. Or it might be the other way around. Picking up the tab is a way to support family. Or maybe, if one party has paid for the airfares, the other is responsible for expenses while you're all together.

When Clive and I visit, or are visited, there are no hard and fast rules. In fact, we've never actually sat down with our children and discussed the subject. Overall, we've done more travelling and invested more in airfares (and lost income while we're away) than we've been visited. And certainly, our children's financial situations have fluctuated. What we are grateful for is that we all share a pretty common attitude towards money and spending.

The following has evolved and works well for our family, but there have been many exceptions along the way.

Parents/grandparents

- We pay for our accommodation when we choose or need to be 'off-site' during visits. This gives us control of the standard, location and facilities.
- We pay for what is of particular importance to us - for example, the costs associated with alone-time activities with individual family members.
- If we've discussed in advance visiting certain attractions, we'll arrive with some, but not all, pre-booked.
- We tend to pay for a fair proportion of meals out for no other reason than Clive is a little too quick with the credit card. I regularly encourage him to allow space for others to gracefully make the move also.

Shared expenses

- Accommodation when we vacation together at another location
- Every second supermarket visit
- Every second fill at the petrol station

Sometimes, of course, things evolve organically. For example, when we visit our U.K. family, we usually holiday together somewhere. We started by sharing a chalet or apartment, but as the grandchildren grew older (and we grew older as well), we progressed to two separate units. There's been no hard and fast rule about how the accommodation account is settled. Sometimes we've split the bill, sometimes we've paid the lot and other times our Distance Family has paid. The latter scenario doesn't sit right with us, but on the other hand, we've done the travelling and invested in the airfares, so we need to allow them the opportunity to contribute. And they also get to choose where we go!

Some readers may baulk at my suggestions. Money is a tricky subject at the best of times. What I am sharing is what has worked for our Distance Family visits. You need to decide what sits right with you, what you can afford and what gives you peace of mind.

Reflection

One price Distance Sons and Daughters pay when they visit their Distance Family is having very little time to see much of their current 'away' country. Most distance parents and grandparents don't think too much about this: they can't imagine there's anywhere you'd rather visit than home.

> "Having lived in Australia for 20 years now, the kids and I have barely seen anything of their home country. We are off to Europe every year [to see her parents]."
>
> Dr Karen Eriksen (Distance Daughter)

One of the few upsides of the COVID-19 pandemic and the inability to visit 'home' was the opportunity for expats and migrants to see more of what's close. I know of many families who have vacationed locally - guilt-free. That's refreshing.

17. VISITS: YOU GO HOME

"When you live abroad... the trip home becomes a mad dash in an expensive hire car with a small boot, on the slowest roads in England... You can't win. If you try to miss out visits to anyone who only wrote to you at Christmas, sure as eggs they'll track you down and ring you up."
Jo Parfitt, 'The Horror of Holidays' in *Forced to Fly*

There is a great deal of truth in Jo's comment. But flipping the scenario on its head, there is also this angle:

"There is no other better way than taking our kids to the place that we, their parents, were born and raised in. They will learn much more by going to places and interacting with people of a different culture."
Madhu Challa, contributor to
Raising the Global Mindset

Visits home by Distance Sons and Daughters can be a minefield of emotions, duties, constraints, expectations, sentimental pondering and harsh realities. You crave the familiar, but each trip home comes with a changing level of connectedness and wavering expectations.

Things move on. You are a changed person since your last visit, but you sense that your Distance Family is locked in a time warp. Your passport shows that you are a national, but that doesn't mirror your identity. Trouble is, rarely is anyone at home aware of your mixed-up thoughts and emotions.

In her book *Unconditional Love*, Jane Isay uses a terrific word: 'obli-cation'. What a fitting word to describe something you want *so* much but simultaneously *dread*. On the one hand you can be yourself, to a certain degree, because you're on home turf and surrounded by your own culture, but on the other hand, you aren't the same person.

Choosing Between

If your parents *and* in-laws live some distance away, how do you decide who to visit, in what order and how often?

> "Intercultural relationships are on the rise. We are juggling visits to our parents' homelands. Three or more countries are involved in intercultural marriages."
>
> Rhoda Bangerter (Distance Daughter)

Furthermore, some parents/grandparents are planners and some aren't; the same can apply to Distance Sons and Daughters. Some personalities want everything sorted in advance, while others work better last minute (or at least they think so).

It's a difficult balancing act for Distance Sons and Daughters when they are faced with choosing between parents. It is sometimes a case of you're damned if you do and damned if you don't. My take on it is that there are many reasons why you might plan things one way or the other, and you're unlikely to please everyone. Hopefully, your parents appreciate your dilemma and don't make unnecessary demands.

How to Even Out Dr Sonia Jaeger's 'All' of 'All or Nothing'

In *Your D.I.Y. Move Guide to Australia*, Robyn Vogels and Hendrika Jooste offer a top tip for when you visit home: "Don't visit each and every family group separately. It is not only exhausting, but you may also eat and drink more than normal!"

There are advantages to staging a big gathering to catch up with a lot of friends in one go, but think of the hosts. I know about this from personal experience - it's like Grand Central Station in our house when the family visits. The message is: don't take the hosts for granted, and factor in being home when it's time to prepare and clean up. Your parents are pleased to support you and want all your friends to turn up, but a little give and take is required.

Out-of-town friends are a problem. You've travelled halfway around the world, and you're surprised they won't drive or fly a few hours to catch up so you don't have to go all over the place. I would suggest this is an unrealistic expectation, even though from your perspective it seems reasonable. It's no reflection on the value of your shared relationship. Everyone has full lives and although you were the best of buddies, and probably still are, people simply can't be all things to everyone all of the time.

Scheduling

You would love your visit home to be a vacation/holiday of sorts. You're yearning to have some downtime. But you also want and need to fit so much in. For some Distance Sons and Daughters, a visit home even comes with a raft of medical check-ups at the likes of the doctor or dentist because it's easier to tick off these responsibilities on home turf.

As much as it goes against the grain to have a holiday with a schedule, there are advantages to being upfront and sharing a good old Excel document in the cloud. Our family does this on Google Drive. We enter our personal 'definites', 'maybes' and the things that 'would be nice'. Final plans are worked from there.

It is hard for us to share our world. Most times... no one back home is interested

Distance Sons, Daughters and grandchildren can feel a sense of loneliness when they visit home. Two things happen:

1. Family and friends brush over your foreign world in favour of local topics relevant to the in-country family and friends. You're proud of your achievements, you've travelled all this way and you're thinking, *Surely someone's interested in my world from my perspective?* It's not that they don't care, they just don't get why you live where you live and why you don't want to come back home. If local family and friends haven't travelled much, the situation can be even more problematic because there's a degree of ignorance about the rest of the world.

2. You're incessantly judged and questioned about your lifestyle choices, not in a curious way, but in what feels like a judgemental way. As Mariam Navaid Ottimofiore explains in *This Messy Mobile Life*, "Such questions or comments... are a well-meaning attempt to relate to a life that is quite frankly unrelatable for them."

So what's the solution? You have three options:

1. Leave talk of your overseas world stored in an imaginary left luggage office at the airport when you arrive. Reclaim it when you check in to fly home. Sound crazy? It can be an entirely reasonable plan of attack.

2. Don't apologise for anything. This is Mariam Navaid Ottimofiore's advice in *This Messy Mobile Life*. Be proud of yourself and what you've achieved.
3. Robyn Vogels and Hendrika Jooste discuss this dilemma in *Your D.I.Y. Move Guide to Australia*. Their advice is to ask questions. "Be interested in what is going on in their lives." This is the most basic conversational tool ever invented and super useful.

This all tells you that there is no right way and no wrong way to deal with family and friends who are disinterested in your world or even critical of your life choices. The chances are that you'll approach each person differently, or you'll find a compromise 'plan of attack' that lands somewhere in the middle.

"Stuff gets stirred up"

These are words from a podcast by Intercultural Strategist Sundae Schneider-Bean. She tells us: "You may find yourself back in old family patterns of 'parent' and 'child' even though you are 40 and have children of your own." Sundae has some good advice here: "Remember, ups and downs are not uncommon when you visit home. They're often a reflection of how you've changed and grown. Welcome them as signposts of appreciation, learning and your own values."

"The hold of the family home on the imagination is difficult to break"

These are confronting but wise words from Dr Barbara Settles, who is a professor of human development and family studies at the University of Delaware. They were penned in 2001, and 20 years on, they are still so true. They sum up why visiting home is such an entanglement of emotions and obligations. Forewarned is forearmed.

The Secret Desires of Distance Parents and Grandparents When They Host

In conversations with distance parents and grandparents about hosting their families, some common niggles always bubble to the surface. These are rarely voiced to visiting family: parents and grandparents don't want to rock the boat. But in the spirit of Dale Carnegie's *How to Win Friends and Influence People*, if you are looking for some easy ways to put a smile on the face of your folks back home, here are some suggestions.

Make your bed

Most distance parents and grandparents love beds that are made - every day and in a timely fashion. The continuous sight of unmade beds is a sort of 'punishment' for the hosts. Parents/grandparents understand there is extra stuff and gear around and that temporarily setting up home can be a little messy. But "I wish they would make their beds" is something I hear all the time.

It is good to remember that during all the months (maybe years) that you aren't there, these rooms are neat and tidy, with an imaginary 'vacant' sign on the door. Your parents and grandparents have rather got used to this level of order. If they always make *their* bed, then making yours is an act of kindness and consideration, even if you aren't that particular at your house.

Hang up wet towels and 'put the seat down'

No more needs to be said.

Go to church: brownie points in heaven

If distance parents/grandparents are regular church goers, they always wish their visiting family would join them (assuming the church is a familiar landmark). Every week, fellow parishioners are asking how their children are. In fact, some parishioners you might not even know may have been praying for you. I have church friends who pray for my Distance Children.

If you sense your parents' faith community is an important part of their life, then joining them at a weekly service could be one of the greatest gifts you give them. This kindness extends to your timekeeping. They don't want to walk into the church with 30 seconds to spare. They know family friends will want to greet you. Think about leaving time for this to happen, and afterwards, try not to be in a hurry to head to the car.

Reflection

Visits home are emotional time bombs. A dose of realism early on is a good idea so you don't over-promise, especially around the amount of time you'll spend with your closest family. They're probably intending to block out their calendar for your entire stay and may need a reality check. Talk frankly, be upfront and include your Distance Family in your planning. They might not be over the moon about your comings and goings, but they'll respect your honesty, know where they stand and have time to adjust.

Once you arrive, they won't be second-guessing what's happening each day - and what's more, their knowledge of your movements will encourage them to carry on with a few of their regular activities. This is a positive outcome for all.

18. VISITS: THEY COME TO YOU

"We've got a nice flat and there's a spare room for you. Do come, you'll love it. And by the way could you bring...?"
Peter Gosling, 'Another Suitcase Another Long Haul' in *Forced to Fly*

Standing in the Arrivals Hall, you take a deep breath. For some, collecting your parents/grandparents is the best day of the year. For others, it's Day One of a countdown until you're back at the airport dropping them off. But at least this time it's on your turf.

Validation

"For migrants whose families do visit them, the experience can be deeply validating for both parties."
Diane Comer, *The Braided River*

When family visit you, they truly begin to understand your new world. Singapore-based international school psychologist Jeff Devens encourages middle-generation expat parents to create opportunities for the family to visit. "Invite them to personally feel the heat, smell the spices, and sense the undercurrents of the culture."

Once they return home, ongoing connections have a new depth. In the case of Devens' Singapore, even when it's winter back home, parents and grandparents can now imagine the humidity and hustle-bustle of this South East Asian metropolis.

If parents and/or other family members are willing and able to visit, this will be special for everyone. Their first-hand understanding and validation of your new home setting will fuel and sustain you through much.

How to Even Out the 'All' of 'All or Nothing' - in the Opposite Direction

As with all visits, be upfront about your concerns *before* the holiday/vacation happens. It is okay to say, "It's been a while since we've all been together, and this is foreign territory for you. We want you to be comfortable, and we don't want to overwhelm you with our noise and mayhem. Let's agree we should speak up and arrange breaks and downtime every so often."

Mix 'n' match outings

One of the themes in *Chapter 1* is 'Alone time - the greatest gift'. Some of my most precious memories of visits in either direction are when we've been able to have a family member (son, daughter, grandchild - anyone!) all to ourselves. It might be as ordinary as a supermarket visit, which is always fascinating in a different country, or a special-treat outing with a grandchild. We once took our cricket-mad grandson into London for a tour of Lord's Cricket Ground. Even now, when Clive sits and watches cricket on television and the familiar ground appears, he thinks back to that day.

Bliss for you might be second-hand/'consignment' shopping with your mum, leaving the men in charge. Bliss for your father might be a round of golf with his new son-in-law, who he'd like to get to know better. Each day, some members of the family may go in a different direction, changing the dynamics at home. And of course, there is the occasional 'everyone together' day.

Illustration by Cath Brew
drawntoastory.com

Mix 'n' match chores

Take turns being in charge of meal preparation and cleaning up so it isn't the same person every day. Allow your mother or mother-in-law to be 'at home' in your kitchen. You might even end up with some ready-made meals in the freezer. The children will love baking with Nana or Grandma.

However, it's good to remember that for some people, hanging out in the kitchen isn't their favourite pastime. They might like cleaning or gardening. So strict rosters aren't always the best solution. Willing volunteers working in their area of choice is always much more successful.

Eat together

"When our family comes together every summer, the most important times are when we can sit and eat together and talk - the evening meal in particular, though we don't always manage it. We all have turns in preparing the food, and I think this is very important. The shared meal is a very practical way of keeping in touch."
Jane Taylor, 'Finding out what is important' in Grandmothers: *The Changing Culture*

When there's lots happening, deciding you'll share as many meals together as possible is a smart way to navigate visits. Try to avoid lining up on the couch in front of the television with a plate on your lap. Sitting around a table is one thing parents/grandparents miss the most. Conversations with good food, a glass of wine and no devices create memories.

"If it's Thursday it's laundry day"

In an earlier life I was a travel agent. For many years I owned a niche travel company specialising in self-catering accommodation in the U.K. and Europe. The likes of villas in Tuscany and Provence were usually reserved for seven nights - from Saturday to Saturday. When clients returned they would tell me about their Sunday to Wednesday outings, packed to the brim with market visits, leisurely gourmet lunches and sightseeing. Then they would explain that by Thursday they were worn out and stayed home to do the washing.

Going out every day all over the place during visits is exhausting (and expensive). It's important for everyone to pace themselves. Have a day at home with nothing more than a good book and of course catch up on that laundry. It's good for the soul to sit still. Call it your vacation 'weekend'.

Planting Seeds

A local distance grandmother friend sent me the following email:

> "I had coffee with a distance grandmother this morning and she was saying really interesting things, having just come back from visiting her nearly two-year-old in Europe. She was heartbroken when the little one didn't want to sit on her knee for a story or allow her to help with feeding and getting dressed, when the child had been quite happy about this during the past visit, nine months ago. My friend realised it was the age/stage the child was at, rather than anything 'going wrong'. The mum kept trying to involve my friend, but the kid wasn't having a bar of it! So the longed-for visit was a big disappointment. I expect you've heard

all sorts of variations! My husband had the same with his distance grandchildren."

Anonymous distance grandmother

We all know that kids go through phases, especially when they're babies and toddlers. If you think grandchild co-operation might be an issue and could upset visiting family, it's best to speak up and warn the visitors. They'll arrive mentally and emotionally prepared, and whatever charming moments the baby or toddler decides to dish out will be an extra bonus.

Pulling these ideas and scenarios together, try to be planners and create modules of how particular days could look, even if those days don't initially have a date next to them. Welcome suggestions from everyone, including your children. The modules are just options and are up for discussion once you know about the weather, energy levels and non-negotiable commitments. It's unlikely everything on the list will be ticked off.

User-friendly (Or Not?) Visitors

We once had a couple stay with us where the husband was unable to entertain himself for five minutes. I was in despair. He wouldn't pick up a book or magazine. He never took himself off for a walk, had a quiet lie-down or sat outside to enjoy my not too bad garden. All he wanted to do was sit at the breakfast bar and chat. He exhausted me.

Some visiting parents and grandparents are more user-friendly than others, and you appreciate their flexibility. The active ones will get themselves around, figure out public transport, stay off-site when it's the wiser option and rent a car or order an Uber to get around. Some visitors are better than others at occupying themselves.

> "I have always been grateful that my dad could drive in any country. Any place we lived in he and my mum would just hire a car and get to know the surroundings. If we had recently moved there, they would leave for a few days (if we were all busy anyway) and explore for us. Then they would turn up with useful information for us: 'Did you know there is a lovely park just over the hill? The kids would love it,' or, 'I found a hardware store in this or that neighbourhood if you need anything.' "
>
> Rhoda Bangerter (Distance Daughter)

If your parents are user-friendly visitors, be glad and grateful - they're not necessarily the norm. And be warned: they may not always stay this way. Jet-setting, aching and ageing bodies and the requirement these days to be super digitally savvy when you travel, may leave them overwhelmed and less inclined to be as flexible as you might wish.

Foreign Bugs - Guilty as Charged

We all know that even in non-pandemic times we pick up bugs when travelling. But it is no fun when those bugs arrive at *your* house. As the heading of this section says, I'm guilty as charged.

At home in New Zealand, I am a fairly healthy specimen. However, put me in an aeroplane and my immune system struggles. I can't remember a long-haul trip when either my husband or I haven't acquired a nagging cough, a chest infection or the dreaded diarrhoea. We have visited many 24-hour clinics and missed days of holiday activity as a result. I once ate some dodgy seafood at a Christmas Eve party in Atlanta. Our Airbnb was on the second storey of a neighbourhood home. I was so pleased the downstairs owners were away as I was up and down all night, causing the ancient floorboards to creak. At one stage I passed out and slid down the hall wall, smashing a hole in it. At the same time, Clive had a seriously high temperature and ghastly flu symptoms. My daughter received an early morning 'help' call on Boxing Day, and I eventually admitted myself to hospital, leaving Clive to fend for himself. A barrage of tests later, it turned out I had severe food poisoning.

Despite eating well and taking lots of immune-building supplements prior to leaving, the 'just in case' course of antibiotics we carry with us always gets taken by one of us. This is no fun for our family, who put up with us running on two cylinders. I am completely sympathetic to Distance Sons and Daughters who are landed with visitors like us. You deserve a medal.

Reflection

Despite all these medical misadventures, unwelcome bugs haven't dominated our stays, and we have never regretted a visit (nor has our family). We've always known when the next visit was due, and those plans have fuelled our Distance Familying engine.

The COVID-19 pandemic changed things for our family and taught us that nothing is guaranteed. On a positive note, I'm grateful that the everyday wearing of face masks has been normalised. I'll never again think twice about wearing one.

19. REPATRIATION IS A BIGGIE

"Give yourself grace."
Marilyn Gardner, founder of Communicating Across Boundaries

Repatriation is a voluntary or involuntary return to your passport country or home country. When this occurs, an expat or migrant becomes what's commonly called a 'repat'.

Some repats are so excited to be returning home they can hardly contain themselves. For others, even though they know it is the right decision, or the only decision for a myriad of reasons, they have emotions ranging from caution to dread. To complicate things, one half of a couple might be overjoyed and the other not so. It is difficult, therefore, to generalise.

There are two stages to the return that directly or indirectly affect Distance Family relationships:

1. The decision
2. Adjusting upon return

The Decision

The decision to return is sometimes yours to make; sometimes it's not. World events, employers, pandemics, contracts, children's education, ageing parents, ill health, visa/work permit issues and retirement are just some of the things that could force or start a return. Sometimes you're ready and sometimes you're not.

It is hard to compare a relatively new expat who's now a homesick, first-time mother-to-be Distance Daughter desperate to be close to mum/mom, to a well-established and settled expat family that's forced to return after decades away because of a job loss caused by a pandemic. Their thinking spaces are worlds apart.

The 'stay or go' dilemma: "should I stay or should I go?"

If you have choices, you may experience the 'stay or go' dilemma.

Melissa Parks is a clinical and health psychologist who counsels clients via her online expat practice at www.intentionalexpat.com. For many years she was a global nomad, and as she explained to me, "I went through mental gymnastics asking myself, *should I go, or should I stay?*" When she became pregnant, she and her Venezuelan partner decided that her hometown, Seattle, U.S.A., was right for the next season of their life.

When deliberating, Melissa had casually mentioned to her mother that she was likely to return home "one day". Every so often her mom would gently remind her: "Don't forget - you said you were coming back." Despite her mother's soft touch, Melissa was conscious that the message was "we want you to come home".

Melissa and her partner followed her own professional advice and made a 'Pros and Cons List'. Even though this showed they had more reasons to *stay* in Spain, they still decided to *go* and be close to family. They told themselves that these decisions were not forever decisions. They were for *that* chapter of their life. Melissa readily admits they may return to Europe for a period so their bilingual son can have the full immersion experience, and several possible retirement locations are regularly bounced about.

There is a saying that goes, 'The grass is always greener on the other side.' Melissa has a great twist on this. Her version goes,

'The grass is greener where you water it.' She is constantly asking herself, *Where do I want to water the grass... now?*

For repat Distance Sons and Daughters, there are three valuable takeaways from Melissa's experiences:

1. A 'Pros and Cons List' has its place, but some decisions we make in life are because they are right to do even if the weights and measures aren't spot on.
2. What might seem like a big decision now may not be a forever decision, so it's good to keep it in perspective.
3. There is value *and* risk in 'planting seeds' with your family ahead of time. In *Chapter 5* I recommended warning family members that you are considering an overseas move because it gives them time to process and adjust to the big news. But if the seed you're planting is *good* news for the recipient, like returning home, once it's said, it can't be unsaid.

Adjusting Upon Return

One of the biggest challenges for repats is dealing with the comments and questions from those at home: before you leave, once you arrive and down the track. Some are well-meaning, some are cynical and others are plain dumb, but the guilty party is often completely unaware how they are coming across.

Once you're back, the extended family may well dismiss everything about your previous global life. They've never done what you've done, and it's a case of 'you don't know what you don't know'. They may also be surrounded by people saying how much you must be pleased to be home, and they assume it must be true. It's like they've wiped your previous life.

It is sensible to accept and tolerate these well-meaning comments and questions (or lack of questions) as part of the repatriation package. They come from a place of having no appreciation of the thought processes and compromises Distance Sons and Daughters have negotiated in deciding to return home.

Melissa Parks offers another perspective here. It's possible that family members are *so* pleased you've returned that they don't want to generate any problems that might cause you to leave again. As Melissa puts it, they are "walking on eggshells". This is a loving regime and a pressure all in one.

Repatriation is a tough gig.

Re-entry or reverse culture shock

"Moving abroad had its challenges; moving back will too."
Esther Twisk, *Expat Magazine*

'Re-entry shock' or 'reverse culture shock' are terms used by Distance Sons and Daughters to describe their psychological experiences: good and bad. Most returnees experience it to a small or large degree during visits, and especially when settling back home. They are technically 'home' and everything should be 'normal', but it isn't. An expat once told me, "The hole closes up behind you when you leave, so when you go back, it's not so easy to slot back in."

Despite the variation in circumstances and different head spaces, there are several definites:

1. You've left special friends and colleagues behind.
2. You've changed.
3. Home has changed, but you still think about it as it once was.
4. Your family and friends may or may not appear to have changed to your way of thinking.

5. Your friends and family have become accustomed to living their lives without you being there.
6. The time spent overseas, and the difference between the cultures you've experienced and that of home, has a big impact.

For the children of Distance Sons and Daughters who have become accustomed to their global world, repatriation can be traumatic, especially if that destination is primarily monocultural and they have been used to multicultural environments. If they've never lived there, their new 'home' is foreign to them. While Distance Sons and Daughters might revel in being back home, some children may feel like fish out of water.

"After years away, I no longer feel at home in England. Everything is familiar, yet everything feels different at the same time. The people, the streets, the smells, they are all the same. Yet, the way I look at them has changed. I see the world differently now to how I saw it five years ago. That is the crux. I have changed, but the people and the places that I left behind have barely changed. I feel like a man without a country, a man without a home. An outsider in my country."

Tom Stevenson, 'The Hardest Part of Living Abroad Nobody Talks About', *Medium*

When Sindhuja Kumar talked about repatriation in *Raising the Global Mindset*, she reminded her readers that children, especially younger ones, are like mirrors and almost always reflect our behaviour: "When they realize that their parents are happy, they can sense the vibe."

Share your hurdles

There are so many things that locals take for granted that have changed since you left. Those at home don't really think about this as they have adjusted over the years. It could have been decades since your parents had to set up a utilities account or figured out the best internet provider.

If you show your vulnerability by admitting you're a little lost, they may begin to appreciate the hurdles you're navigating. They may understand that you have changed, that home for you isn't the comfortable and familiar place it is for them. It's good for your family to understand this. There may be some who aren't sympathetic, but you will have figured out who they are a long time ago.

Find a new tribe

The bunch of friends you had before you left won't be the same group you mix with when you return. Just as Distance Sons and Daughters worked at finding friends in a new location, home requires the same attention.

Margot Andersen is the founder of Insync Network Group in Australia and hosts a podcast called *Boomeranging*. She supports repatriating Australians. The words she uses to describe repatriation are isolation, surprise and feeling an outsider in your own country. Her message is: "Arrive well, work well and live well."

Margot maintains that the first few months are the hardest, and one of her key pieces of advice is to find a tribe of other expatriates. It is common to underestimate how much Distance Sons and Daughters change while being overseas. The mental demands of repatriating are like throwing oneself in a washing machine.

Anna Seidel is a Distance Daughter and a global mobility trainer. She is an American living in Germany. She states it can take up to

18 months to feel settled after repatriating, and each member of the family has their own timeline. I support Anna's recommendation of Craig Storti's book *The Art of Coming Home*. Storti explains that familiarity is the key. Once places, people and routines are familiar and predictable, home begins to truly feel like home. Therefore, patience is an essential ingredient.

My advice about finding a tribe is don't take your foot off the accelerator just because you're home. Treat home with the same fervour as you did your foreign location. You've learnt so much. You've changed and you've grown, and it's an exciting opportunity to quietly sift through the old friends, find new ones and reinvent your social circle.

Reflection

Foreboding concerns about repatriation aren't just confined to Distance Sons and Daughters. Here's my story.

I recall a time when my daughter Lucy rang home from Bangkok and said they were seriously looking at moving to New Zealand. The pollution of Bangkok had them concerned for the health of our grandson. Questions about house prices and rental fees were fired at us. In many ways we were delighted, but part of me was saying, "Oh boy, my life will never be the same." I was used to life as it was. As it turned out, talk of the move was short-lived, and a picket fence move to Atlanta with a job transfer/promotion won them over. But for a brief moment, they threw my life into disarray. So my message is this: don't assume everyone is over the moon about every aspect of your return. There can be mixed emotions on both sides.

20. FINANCIAL COMINGS AND GOINGS

"Financial decisions are influenced by our attitudes, which are highly influenced by cultural issues, including family, ethnicity, gender, and socioeconomic status."
Sonya L. Britt, *The Journal of Consumer Affairs*

Distance Family intergenerational financial support, in either direction, can be both problematic and a blessing. Once again, there's no manual. Author Ana McGinley, who features in the next chapter, reminds us that older parents and grandparents of Distance Sons and Daughters grew up in a time when speaking about money was considered crass. Therefore, discussions around the to and fro of money can be rather prickly.

In this chapter I'm not talking about who pays for the groceries during a visit; by now you will have figured out what works for your family on that front. But what about the bigger picture such as loans and other financial support? There is little documented about how this affects Distance Families. From my discussions with all generations of Distance Families, there are some important lessons to be learnt.

To Receive

Financial support from your parents and/or grandparents can take many forms. It can be complicated for you and complicated for them.

Loans and the like

When financial situations are strained for Distance Sons and Daughters, the perceived financial safety net of home can seem even further away. You don't want to be in this situation. If you have a pressing or urgent financial problem and all you can think about is solving the immediate issue, that's understandable. You may, reluctantly or otherwise, look to your parents or grandparents for support. Few parents or grandparents are prepared for this scenario, and they will often struggle to know what's the right thing to do.

Too often, loans aren't repaid. In fairness, parents and grandparents may not be firm enough or official enough about the repayment terms. They are betwixt and between and sometimes not in complete agreement themselves. There may even be guilt at play - about parenting shortcomings in the past, for instance. As a result, when money changes hands, the terms are vague or opaque.

Just know that if your parents or grandparents say to you, "Pay us back when you can," what they *actually* mean is, "We expect to be paid back." They silently hope you respect their position, commit to a repayment plan (without being asked) *and* keep to the plan. When you diligently follow through, they are so relieved. If you don't, the loan becomes a lingering bad smell of their parenting. Retirement savings may have been depleted, perhaps leaving them vulnerable for when you're not there 'to do' for them. They feel they've failed as parents because their son or daughter hasn't done the right thing. If there *is* a repayment problem, it's best to speak up, even if your pride is bruised. You'll more than likely find them incredibly understanding. Burying the situation, or worse still, forgetting about it, is damaging.

A grandparent couple I interviewed for my research admitted they had naively "lent" their Distance Family money and had never been repaid. They later financed a visit to New Zealand from the

U.K. They regretted they hadn't been firmer about the loan terms and felt they'd probably been too generous considering their own financial situation. As the grandfather quietly admitted, "Thanks to that decision, we won't be putting down a new carpet any time soon."

Financial gifts

My research has taught me that parents and grandparents come with their own set of financial values, or you could better describe them as unwritten rules. These rules can appear set in stone and then one day they surprise you - and probably themselves - by changing them. Maybe they'd always expected their Distance Children to pay their own way when visiting home, and you were totally accepting of that. Then one day there's a left-field offer to pay for some airfares. Maybe their situation has changed. Perhaps they have less appetite or stamina for travel. Who knows? It's hard to know exactly where you stand. When parents and grandparents make these decisions, just know that the offers are sincere, that they truly want to help.

To Give

As parents age, they hopefully open up a little about their financial situation. Questions about wills and powers of attorney may need to be broached, and it's always better if these discussions are initiated by the seniors. We all hope our parents have the resources to retain their independence and not 'go without', but life can be cruel and this isn't always the case.

There may come a day when you sense you'd like to financially support your parents - or maybe they need you to. It's important that any arrangements you make are crystal clear and that if you are a couple, both of you are on the same page about the decisions you make.

Offering such support may well result in some tricky conversations, but time will help them to digest it. There's wisdom in setting up a regular commitment rather than a one-off. You could offer to pay for a cleaner, a gardener or a local car ride service. The secret is to ensure your parent or parents retain their dignity. If they are hesitant, suggest a one-off trial. Explain that you want their input, that it's important the service provider is right for them, that your parents feel comfortable with them in their home. In other words, show your parents respect by involving them and asking for their opinion.

It may take time for your parents to adapt to the new arrangements, so don't be too anxious if feedback is vague. Allow your parents the time to process this new experience. They need to grieve their loss of independence and adjust to a new reliance on others.

If you are thinking your financial contributions should be offset (reimbursed) when it's time to settle your parents' estate, make it crystal clear - in writing - to all parties/beneficiaries before you pay a cent. Otherwise you may end up being one of those families who fight tooth and nail over an estate - and that is not what your parents would want.

Comparisons Aren't Wise

Each set of parents and/or grandparents has their own financial values that need to be honoured and respected. The in-laws may offer financial support to you that does not sit well with your parents' values. This can create a 'them and us' situation. For example, one set of parents may choose to help fund their grandchildren's university education, while the other grandparents would never consider this - they may see your children's education as *your* responsibility. And of course, *you* might support your parents and parents-in-law differently. That's perfectly okay - it's your prerogative.

Trying to keep things 'even' can create issues for all concerned. The best approach is to give with good grace and be grateful for what comes your way - and leave it at that.

Reflection

There is value in reflecting upon the intentions behind any financial support. There are two likely scenarios, and they can apply in *either* direction:

1. Financial support because one party needs it
2. Financial support that gives one or both parties joy but isn't essential: giving for the sake of giving

As distance parents and grandparents, Clive and I have occasionally volunteered to offer financial support to our Distance Family. Sometimes it's solved a temporary problem, sometimes it was something important to us and made for a left-field surprise. All arrangements are private and not a topic of discussion with the rest of our family.

There are no rules that say offers of support need to be loans or gifts, or that the arrangements should be made public or kept more private. The goal is to have terms that are clear and agreed - and to stick to them.

Some distance parents and grandparents who invest financially in their adult children or grandchildren are under the sad illusion that their family 'owes them'. In *Rules of Estrangement*, Joshua Coleman asserts that the exchange rate of parental investment has weakened over the last 50 years. "Parents, for better or worse, can no longer demand contact as a return on time and money spent." I'm with Coleman.

Finally, a personal story from decades ago. When I unexpectedly acquired the title of solo mother, my parents offered to pay for the lawn mowing service at my house. It was one less bill to budget for every week. The arrangement was clear-cut (excuse the pun). They knew where they stood, and I knew where I stood. Every fortnight, I felt my parents' love descend upon me when the tradesperson pulled up in my driveway. When these sorts of arrangements are successful, in either direction, it is a win-win for all.

21. DECLINE AND CARING AT A DISTANCE

"Age does not change the person you are. It may change the life you lead, but it does not alter the inner being that is you."
Ana McGinley, *Parental Guidance: Long Distance Care for Aging Parents*

"Most of us come into the world viewing our parents as healthy, strong and everlasting. As we grow, and as they age, the naïve feeling that they are a perpetual part of our lives fades. Their hearing weakens, their gait slows, their memories dim, and for adult children the experience can provoke feelings of anger, anxiety, fear and frustration."
Alia E. Dastagir, *USA Today*

This is the first of two chapters about coping with and caring for elderly family from afar. The next chapter will look at *Death at a Distance and Settling Affairs*. Unsurprisingly, research confirms that this precarious season of life is one of the toughest for Distance Sons and Daughters to cope with. It is so much harder when distance is involved: not only are you navigating uncharted territory, you find yourself questioning why you live where you do.

Although I talk mostly about parents and grandparents in these chapters, much of this applies to *any* close family member. Losing a sibling, close aunt or special cousin - they are all impactful.

The Mediating Anxious Feelings Pie

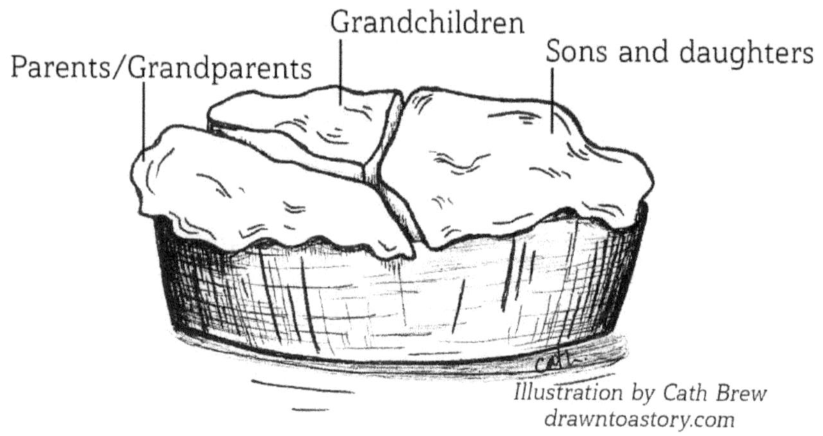

Illustration by Cath Brew
drawntoastory.com

In *Chapter 11*, I talked about The Distance Family Thinking Pie. This is an imaginary pie, sliced in three - the size of each slice representing how much each generation (grandparents, parents and grandchildren) spend time and energy *thinking* about each other. Distance grandparents earn the biggest slice and do the most thinking.

We could therefore assume that distance grandparents also consume the biggest slice of an imaginary *Mediating Anxious Feelings Pie*. Surprisingly, the grandparents take a very close runner-up position. With their never-ending guilt about left-behind family, Distance Sons and Daughters take the biggest slice here. There's no escaping it. Somewhere along the way you'll be served a generous portion of that pie, especially when your parents start to decline. It will be difficult and sad. Guilt will be your unwelcome companion and anxiety levels will be at an all-time high.

> "Despite my being one of five siblings and living the furthest away, it was left almost entirely to us and our children [to tend to her distance parents]."
>
> Frances (Distance Daughter in Wales with family in Canada). Cited in an article by *Medium* writer Katarzyna.

Another Key Resource

During my research I found an excellent support book: *Parental Guidance: Long Distance Care for Aging Parents*, by Ana McGinley. Ana has a medical background, which complements my anthropological approach. She offers excellent advice about common chronic medical issues, legal/financial issues and dealing with hospitals and authorities in person and from afar. I'd recommend owning the e-book version rather than the paperback so you'll always have it with you if you've had to hop on a plane in a hurry.

The Autumn (Fall) of Life

Marilyn R. Gardner is a public health nurse and writer who lives in Boston. She was raised in Pakistan, where her New England-born parents lived and worked for 35 years. Marilyn went on to raise her own children in Egypt. In her writings she often refers to autumn (fall) and the beauty that can be found in New England during this season. Her parents have long since passed, but each year, when autumn comes around, Marilyn's visits to New England remind her of what her parents left behind and how this area has become infused into her life, despite her not being raised there. In an article titled *The Autumn of My Parents*, she says: "Removing this part of who I am, of where my parents were raised and what went in to making them the people they are, would sever the tapestry and it would be incomplete."

Marilyn's writings led me to thinking about how the season of autumn is such a powerful resting place for thoughts of our declining parents and grandparents. Autumn is a natural, predictable occurrence, just as the decline and eventual passing of our parents, grandparents and other close family members is to be expected. There is beauty in the leaves of every hue as they change their colour. Marilyn's autumn analogy resonates here. Leaves cling to their branches, determined to 'hang around' for as long as they can. Then a winter wind arrives and they can cling on no longer, landing on the ground to eventually be blown away. When the going gets tough and you're coping with declining family from afar, occasionally rest your thoughts for a moment in the beauty of autumn.

"Do What's Right for You"

"Older people have already had the experience of their own parents or relatives aging and needing help. This experience will have formed their own opinions about how they would like to live in their later years."
Ana McGinley, *Parental Guidance: Long Distance Care for Aging Parents*

A conversation with my mother prompted me to include the line "Do What's Right for You". Today, as I write this, she is attending an extra special Happy Hour for the residents and staff at her lifestyle village. They are 'farewelling' the sales and marketing manager, Rosalie. Rosalie is well known for her patience and grace when supporting families through decisions about selling the family home and moving into a retirement village. Her counsel to potential new arrivals has always been, "Do what's right for you." Today she is leaving her position to move closer to family as she is about to become a first-time grandmother. Rosalie is taking her own advice and 'doing what's right' for her.

I share this story as there is much we can learn. There is wisdom in Distance Sons and Daughters standing back and embracing this line as much as possible. If parents are pleased about their plans, so should you be. Ironically, when you decided to live overseas and maybe family at home weren't so positive, oh how you wished their cry had been, "Do what's right for you."

Encouraging and helping your parents to plan for their senior years is sometimes easier said than done - and is it your role anyway? Some parents are planners and might even take you by surprise and announce they're moving to a retirement complex or they've prepaid for their funeral. You might not be ready for that transition.

Some parents don't want change, and that's their choice. They crave their independence, are willing to doggedly tolerate the physical and financial demands of maintaining their current home and snap back at any mention of downsizing. This type of resilient stance may be what's right for them, and many cope incredibly well.

Another consideration is culture. As I mentioned in *Who Isn't Featured in This Book*, I am mostly focussing on Western, English-speaking nationalities and how they approach Distance Familying. Carolina Porto, who has written global mobility books in Portuguese and Spanish, told me in an email conversation that talk of retirement villages and care homes would be the worst outcome for a Latino Distance Family. 'Doing what's right' for one is not necessarily 'doing what's right' for another. Carolina emphasises the need to start conversations with parents and grandparents early, so there is plenty of time to prepare emotionally and financially.

Making sense of their decisions - because it's helpful

"Most of us have an inherent need to make things right for our parents should they become sick or frail. We don't want to see them deprived of the help and health care they need. Sometimes we want this more than they want it themselves."
Ana McGinley, *Parental Guidance: Long Distance Care for Aging Parents*

Laura Carstensen is a professor of psychology at Stanford University. She is the founding director of the Stanford Center on Longevity. Her research has focused on how motivational changes influence cognitive processing. In other words, why do seniors want something different from what *you* might like for them or think is right? Quite simply, as people age, their *emotional needs* become more important than *other needs*. They would rather remain in a less than suitable family home than cope with moving.

These findings are further clarified by Dr Stephen Golant. His thinking is along the same lines but frameworked around the 'residential normalcy' theoretical model and evaluates their residential **comfort** and residential **mastery**. In simple terms, older people make housing decisions based on two sets of criteria:

Is this a comfortable, appealing, hassle-free place to live? (**comfort**)

Do I feel competent and in control of my life living here? (**mastery**)

Answering yes to both is the best scenario. However, the answer is often yes to one and no to another - but the yes answer is definite enough to balance out the no.

As a son or daughter, you can clearly see the "no" answer, and that concerns you. But as Dr Golant points out: "Older people can live in places with split personalities." They weigh up the good with the bad, make some compromises, tweak how they navigate the day-to-day and accept that things aren't perfect. Overall, they would rather leave things as they are.

As Susan Williams, a journalist for *Booming Encore*, puts it: "Life is just riddled with risks. Our challenge is to be able to accept this not only for ourselves but sometimes also for the people we care about."

A word of caution here. Parents can be adamant that, for example, they will never sell the family home and downsize. Then out of the blue they have a 360-degree change of mind. So what happened? Maybe they have friends who've made the move, and that's made them think. Maybe they've grown weary of maintenance tasks. When their thoughts about **comfort** and **mastery** take a sharp turn, allow them the space to transition and change their mind with grace.

Negotiated Commitments

"Caregiving between family members is not a straightforward product of fixed rules of obligation, but the result of longstanding processes of negotiation based on a combination of normative guidelines and negotiated commitments."

Professor Baldassar and colleagues, *Families Caring Across Borders*

In *Families Caring Across Borders*, Professor Baldassar explains that *who* provides support to *whom*, how, when and why is characterised by combinations of capacity, sense of obligation and the history of negotiated commitments.

For example, some families consider it normal for the distance mother/grandmother to visit her daughter when a baby is due.

In other families, the last person a Distance Daughter (let alone her partner) wants is a mother fussing about the place. What is a negotiated commitment at one household isn't necessarily the same at another.

The Sandwich Generation Club

"The world has never had so many people living beyond our evolved biological warranty period."
Colin Farrelly, *The Journals of Gerontology*

You can find yourself being a member of the sandwich generation club at a relatively early age and hang around the club for a long time. I know seniors in their 70s living in retirement villages who still have an elderly parent in care. At the same time, one generation down (maybe you) could also be looking for support. Your parents' generation is the first to widely experience a combination of generational *and* geographical responsibility this late in life.

Looking to the future, if your distance parents have reached their 90s, and you, their Distance Son or Daughter, are in your late 60s or 70s, you might feel too old to travel back home. This is a scary prospect for those of us left behind!

As time goes on, becoming a member of the Sandwich Generation Club is something few people will escape. This is best viewed as a by-product of generations living for longer, but as we need to spread ourselves around, near and far, it comes at a cost.

Single child overwhelm

So far, I have written about family situations where siblings share the support of declining parents. But for many, as an only child, there is no such luxury. The burden can be great.

Australian-based Dr Karen Eriksen was one of two children, but her brother died tragically in a car crash at the age of 18. Her mother cared for her increasingly demented father at home in Germany for 13 years. "It was heartbreaking to watch his decline from afar and on our visits," said Karen, "and even worse not to be able to help and support my mother more." Karen admits dreading their weekly Skype calls. The technology was always challenging but worse was seeing her housebound mother lose her sparkle as life closed in on her. Visits to Germany were numerous and the overdraft exploded. When her father finally died it was another dash to Europe, a quickly arranged funeral and Karen "bundled" up her mother and brought her permanently back to Australia. As the only child, it was tough, but at least they are all now on the same continent.

Single-child families are on the increase for all manner of reasons. I can't help but wonder how these children will cope when they're left in charge. We can learn much from the repercussions of China's 'one' law. This has resulted in two to three generations of single-child families. So many older people and so few younger ones to care for them. If you are interested in China's regime, I can highly recommend *One Child* by Mei Fong for an insightful read.

Spousal bonds

In her book *Parental Guidance: Long Distance Care for Aging Parents*, Ana McGinley has a topic called 'Till Death Do Us Part'. She explains that if your parents have been married for decades, bonds of loyalty (and even servitude) can be hard to loosen. Their vows are sacrosanct, and it can be heart-wrenching to watch one parent care devotedly for the other when the going gets extra tough. Admitting defeat when caregiving gets too much can be more than they can handle. Ana has some extremely useful advice here: "Supporting the individuals, rather than seeing the couple as a single unit, will promote an individual acceptance of the situation from their own personal perspective and relieve the unreasonable expectations of 'till death do us part'."

"Do What's Right for You".... BUT

"Understanding the psychology behind why accepting help may be difficult for an older person is essential for all family and professional care providers."
Ana McGinley, *Parental Guidance: Long Distance Care for Aging Parents*

Maybe you took a step back and graciously accepted the "do what's right for you" cry, but things have moved on. Now you feel your parent or parents aren't doing so well and need additional support and/or they're definitely not living in the best place. Perhaps, in your opinion, the answer to *both* Golant's *residential comfort* and *residential mastery* considerations is "no". All of this can happen quickly. Distance Sons and Daughters who only see a face on a screen and have no assurances of what is happening elsewhere are between a rock and a hard place.

Amy Scott is the founder of Nomadtopia. During a podcast, we talked about the stress of travelling home and observing parents or grandparents who have declined significantly but no one around you seems to have noticed. Amy quoted a case where the elderly mother was doing a terrific coverup job on the local family, and it was the visiting distance sibling who saw all the signs and ended up with the difficult task of pointing out to the rest of the family their mother's tell-tale signs of decline. Staying with distance parents or grandparents can be revealing: it may expose their vulnerability and how they are unable to 'perform' 24/7.

Strategies from a distance

What can you do? First, take a deep breath. Your life and your relationship with your parents are moving to a different space and are unlikely to return to where they were. It is going to take time, patience, fortitude and love.

"Your life and your relationship with your parents are moving to a different space and are unlikely to return to where they were. It is going to take time, patience, fortitude and love."

Here are some practical suggestions:

"How ARE you?"

If things are declining on the home front, a useful early warning sign is that they won't be out and about much. You'll find they're more available, which can be helpful if you have a tricky time-zone connection. If you sense something isn't right at home, start conversations with a slow and deliberate, "How ARE you?" Then pause and wait for a response. Don't give up the first time if you don't receive what you feel is a full answer. Say the same thing next time you call. Hopefully they'll open up. Or you might need to read between the lines - they may hate feeling less able and find it difficult to talk about.

Quantity over quality

If your communication routines currently revolve around *quality* once-a-week video chats, this is the stage where I suggest you gradually switch your communication routines and focus on *quantity*. Don't save everything up for once a week. Slowly but surely, tweak things a little. Consider the following:

- Increasing the frequency of calls
- Shorter calls, but more often
- Being prepared for more one-sided small-talk about a lot of everyday things

Seniors are often slower in the mornings. They may not have slept well and may experience pain and discomfort 'loosening up' their bodies each morning. Rushing around first thing is a no-go territory. They may avoid the 8.30am doctor's appointment and go for the 11am slot instead. What's more, that might be enough activity for one day. These slow mornings can be tricky for Distance Sons and Daughters with less than helpful time-zone connections. If you normally connect with your distance parents during your parents' mornings, ask them, "Am I ringing too early? Is this hard for you?"

Ask your sibling/s or a close friend or relative

Have some quiet conversations on the side. Share your concerns. Ask for the opinions of others and be open to their responses. They may be extremely pleased to hear from you and grateful they aren't the only one thinking this way, or they may see nothing wrong. The latter is tough and you may need to keep observing for a bit longer.

Appoint a Family Manager

Ana McGinley recommends that if you aren't an only child and you have siblings back home, appoint a Family Manager. Ideally, the sibling comes with a natural practical streak and will take on the role of the gatherer and dispenser of information about your parents or any other ageing family member. Most families have one person who surfaces and somehow ends up, happily or otherwise, with this role. As Ana notes: "Most importantly ensure that the Family Manager knows that you appreciate them and the difficult role they have been allocated."

To Travel or Not to Travel

I told a story in *Being a Distance Grandparent* that was shared with me during a visit with a New Zealand distance grandparent couple. I am sharing it again because it touched us all. Their Distance Son and Daughter-in-law, who live in Germany, told them there would "always be money for an airfare". In other words, if they needed to come home in a hurry, money wouldn't be an obstacle - they would make it happen somehow. This simple but important assurance meant so much. We were all in tears.

During pandemics, assurances of 'being there' are sometimes difficult to deliver, but even stating that if you could, you would, is of great comfort.

If your parents are in their 50s or 60s, you are less likely to have had to cope with a rushed trip home, and that's a blessing. However, once your parents reach their 70s or 80s, I recommend that you budget, build up some savings and always have an airfare (plus some) set aside. Make it a priority over other outgoings, if at all possible. This will give you peace of mind. You will find Ana McGinley's book helpful here. Her medical background offers much wisdom, particularly when you are gathering facts and deciding whether or not to travel.

The 'out-of-town expert with the briefcase'

Clive, my accountant husband, isn't one of those boring types with no personality who sits in an office poring over figures all day. Yes, he does 'the books', but he is also a friend, mentor and sometimes even marriage guidance counsellor to his clients. For decades he has been self-employed, with hundreds of clients who are mainly small traders and business owners, like plumbers, builders, hairdressers, and so on - lots of ordinary, hardworking folk. Sometimes Clive becomes the trustee of a family trust for one of his clients. When the parents become elderly, the 'fun' begins. I'll ask Clive how his day has been and he'll say, "Oh, fine. Been dealing with an 'out-of-town expert with the briefcase'." By now, I know exactly what he means.

An overseas sibling has turned up for a visit; perhaps their mum or dad (his client) isn't so well. Prior to this, the local sibling is the one who's been doing their best to care for the parent/s (as an official or unofficial Family Manager), making all the on-the-spot decisions on behalf of or together with the parent. They've driven them to appointments, become an expert about their medications, 'been there' and listened to the same old stories over and over again. That local sibling has made many observations as the parents declined and has an intimate knowledge of their needs. They've also done their best to keep the overseas sibling informed, but their load has been great.

The 'out-of-town expert with the briefcase' (the overseas sibling) arrives in town and bosses the local hardworking sibling, issuing instructions, pushing for fast decisions and questioning everything. The declining parent/s are naturally delighted to see their Distance Child and make them the star of the moment. Now the local sibling has to 'deal' with their brother or sister as well. Most times, the parent/s are oblivious to all that's going on in the background.

Deep down, the abroad sibling may be hurting. They haven't 'been there' in the way their in-country sibling has, and often their way of making up for this void is to 'take over' - especially if they are the oldest child. This is fertile ground for sibling conflict and, worse still, estrangement. As Karl Pillemer explains in *Fault Lines*, families have "taken for granted expectations" about how family should help out when needed, but not everyone is on the same page.

'Deeper things under the surface'

This title is not my invention. It headed up an article by theologian, teacher, author and lay priest Ronald Rolheiser. The article describes the 'out-of-town expert' situation between two sisters and their ageing mother - from the local sister's perspective. The local daughter, who has done the hard graft, resents it when the Distance Daughter strolls in and gets all the attention. But Rolheiser gently reminds the reader of an important point: the local daughter has gained something the Distance Daughter may never achieve - a deep bonding with her mother.

The crux of the article is that the intimacy of relationships is sustained and deepened by 'being there'. As Rolheiser says: "In all our relationships, we cannot make promises as to how we will always feel, but we can make promises to always be faithful, to show up, to be there, even if we are only talking about the weather, our favourite sports team, the latest television fare, or our own tiredness." The local daughter has been doing this, day in and day out.

This is tough to read when you're the Distance Son or Daughter. But I am here to tell you it *doesn't* always have to be this way. You can write your own family narrative. You can do great things from a distance; it just takes creativity, time and a bucketload of commitment to all parties.

To support my stance, *New York Times* political and cultural commentator David Brooks wrote about "nonobvious" lessons to achieve deeper conversations. He cites mediator Adar Cohen's term, 'gem statements': powerful but subtle comments that bind relationships. The example Cohen provides is apt for our distance siblings topic: "Even when we can't agree on Dad's medical care, I've never doubted your good intentions. I know you want the best for him."

Being 'the out-of-town expert with the briefcase' is never a good thing. Compassionate visits are not a vacation, and catching up with old friends should be an extra bonus. This is a time for 'being there', as boring, humdrum, disturbing and confronting as that might be. At the same time, recognise the efforts of your local sibling and give them a well-earned break if you can. Ahead of your visit, ask them to list all the ways you can best help.

Reflection

When I researched and wrote this chapter, its timing coincided with pandemic lockdowns, nursing Clive through a knee replacement operation and supporting my elderly mother. It's tough when people you love aren't running on all cylinders. But I learned a lot, and the journey has helped me be a better wife and daughter.

I hope this chapter has given you some clarity about how your folks might be thinking and how you can support them in a way that *works for them*. As my friend and Distance Daughter Rhoda Bangerter said, "Caring for an ageing parent from abroad is about listening to what they say and thinking outside the box as to how you can help fill any need they mention. It is also about asking questions, delving a bit deeper into a problem they are explaining."

Whether family are near or far, all we can do is our best.

22. DEATH AT A DISTANCE AND SETTLING AFFAIRS

"When major life events occur like weddings, graduations, and, sadly, even funerals, the meaning of connection changes and its importance elevates."
Neustaedter et al., *Connecting Families*

As an expat or migrant, you'll find a limited number of tools available to prepare yourself for the inevitable when a close family member dies back home. I have come to the conclusion that Distance Sons and Daughters - in a way that is different from their siblings back home - need to take themselves on a personal learning journey: *ahead* of when they need to know the answers.

There are five reasons why this is important:

1. No amount of forethought will really help when you get 'that call'.
2. Important decisions *have* to be made.
3. You may also be getting on a plane in a hurry and your life has been turned upside down.
4. If you have children, you're still a parent, and they need as much of you as you can share around.
5. You'll be grieving and this is tough.

Your most valuable resource is your parent or loved one. In *Being a Distance Grandparent* I encourage seniors to start planning their funeral ahead of time by setting up a digital vault of preferences. This is a continuous work-in-progress folder in the likes of Google Drive that they keep adding to. All the family can access it when the parents are ready. They note wishes about their final days and the funeral arrangements. I even go as far as suggesting they choose hymns, write the service and draft a eulogy. What a gift that would be.

One of the most time-hungry tasks when preparing for a funeral is scanning old photographs and digging through mobile phones and computers for prized family snaps to feature in a video collage. If you as the Distance Son or Daughter are a whizz with technology, maybe someone at home can start the scanning and load the photos onto the drive, and you can take it from there.

If you are able to broach the subject of a digital vault with your parents, you can be sure, when the time comes, you've done what they really wanted.

In tandem, it also pays to have an understanding of your family's legal, ritual/tradition and/or religious requirements, particularly as they apply in your home country. An excellent place to start is the website of your national Funeral Directors Association. Here are some:

Australia: www.afda.org.au

Canada: www.fsac.ca

Ireland: www.iafd.ie

New Zealand: www.fdanz.co.nz

South Africa: www.nfda.org.za

United Kingdom: www.nafd.org.uk

U.S.A. www.rememberingalife.com

Another useful tool is Ana McGinley's book *Parental Guidance: Long Distance Care for Aging Parents*, which covers legal issues and, importantly, caring for yourself after a parent passes. She also reminds readers about the importance of ensuring their own affairs are in order.

When the Time Is Near

"Dealing with the death of your parents at a distance is hard, and no matter that we console ourselves with the platitudes of 'I could have been in the next room and not been there when he died' or 'she wanted us to see the world' or 'I went back as much as possible,' there is still a lingering guilt that we were on the other side of the world when death dealt its hand. But because human nature is as it is, we grieve and then slowly let the pieces of our life, that one we have chosen, envelop us as we learn to manage and live with the sorrow."

Apple Gidley, *The Telegraph*

Time zone blessings

When I met Melbourne-based relocation expert Robyn Vogels online, she was in a difficult space. She had personal health challenges with an operation on the horizon, and her dad was dying back in South Africa. She was reading *Being a Distance Grandparent* and told me, "The timing of your book is striking a particular chord with me, but also providing comfort in helping me be at peace with him being a distance grandad."

Even though time zones can exacerbate feelings of loneliness and anxiety, they *can* be a blessing during the last days. As Robyn explains, "Being awake at a time when my South African family is asleep, I can be a distance chat line for the sick or those who can't sleep. Living in this vast time zone, I feel like I grieve alone. Sure I have my immediate family around me, but to be awake in the South African time zone means it's the middle of the night in Australia, shrouded in darkness. Living in a time zone that is ahead of the rest of the world, I almost feel like I am ahead of the process compared to my siblings. In the light of a new day, there are new emotions and by the time my older brother called me at 1pm my time, 9am his time, I had already got over my 'cry' of the day."

I have some personal experience here. I slept over in the hospital room when my dad's death was imminent. My mother was also there, and when I woke in the middle of the night, she was sleeping soundly, which was a blessing. I felt very alone listening to Dad's laboured breathing. I remembered that a close cousin and his wife were visiting Paris, and in the dark, I texted them an update. It was daytime for them and they responded immediately. That text message was a great comfort at a time when I needed not to feel so alone.

Back to my online conversation with Robyn. She continued: "Given COVID, I cannot travel, but that has not stopped me. I support my brother by phoning him when times are tough and letting him vent, cry or chat. I made a photo collage of us all that is hanging next to my dad in bed. I buy groceries online for my mom and have them delivered. There are things we can do from a distance."

A few months down the track, Robyn's dad passed.

Funerals Are Important

"The process now is not [about] caring for your parent. [They have passed.] It is about looking after yourself as you grieve."
Ana McGinley, ***Parental Guidance: Long Distance Care for Aging Parents***

There are so many considerations when making a decision to return home for a funeral: money, time, left-behind family, work and more. If you can make it home, I recommend it. Attending a funeral can significantly help the grieving process.

I lost my dad 14 years ago and I remember events so clearly. It was a blessing he lived nearby. The weekday funeral meant time away from work. The many friends and acquaintances who took time off overwhelmed me. Some had never met my dad: they came for *me*. It meant so much. Since then, I've become more diligent in attending funerals of people I directly *and* indirectly know. I want to support my friends in the same way my friends supported me. Whenever or wherever you can, attend funerals.

Before the COVID pandemic, if you couldn't return home, the only way to be part of the service was to ask a friend or family member to record it. Those days have gone, and many of us have since attended funerals - in person or online via Zoom - where there was a professional videographer present. Virtual funerals are here to stay and are a positive from the pandemic. This is a topic you may want to raise ahead of time with your siblings back home. At a recent funeral I attended, the professional videographer told me his services were in high demand. Business is brisk. Videographers might need to be one of the first calls.

Afterwards

Friends and family - a lolly scramble

A lolly scramble is a children's party game in which an adult throws fistfuls of wrapped lollies (confectionary) into the air and the children scramble around to catch them. When someone close dies, how friends and family react can be something of a lolly scramble. Let me explain.

When times are tough, we crave *different* kinds of support. Friends who support you in times of need tend to fall into three camps, regardless of whether they are local or live back home:

1. Some friends will somehow know exactly what you need, even when you don't always know yourself.
2. Others mean well but are a nuisance and a burden. You feel that *you're* the one who has to prop *them* up and assure them all's fine.
3. The last group quietly and awkwardly ignore you (or they might say they didn't want to 'bother' you). This might be perfect for you. Or not.

All three categories are perfectly normal, and it's unwise to make judgements. We can't be everything to everyone all of the time, and neither can our friends and family. When circumstances are reversed and a friend or relative is experiencing loss, the chances are that *we* will also chop and change between 1, 2 and 3.

So when times are tough, it can be a bit of an unplanned lolly scramble. We might have friends and family who hit the spot perfectly, others who are over-the-top pains and a few who surprise us by their absence.

"After the last casserole has been delivered"

None of us know how we will cope with the grief of losing a loved one. It isn't a process with an end date. There will always be a void, and that void is okay. Your local friends may have never met your distance parent, and that can make it a very lonely space. The first of everything (Christmas, birthday, Father's Day, and so on) are the toughest, and it's even harder from a distance when you can't visit a gravesite for a quiet moment of reflection.

Australians Kirsty Rice and Nikki Moffitt are seasoned expats who deliver the popular podcast Two Fat Expats. They have both lost parents and don't hesitate to share their grief that even years later is still very real. Referring to a TED Talk by writer/podcaster Nora McInerny, Kirsty talked about how it is "after the last casserole is delivered". As she explained, the world thinks it's time for you to move on, and we don't make those stipulations on anyone else or anything else in our life, but we kind of do with grief. I loved the analogy of the quiet, empty void where people expect you to stop talking about your recent loss. As Nikki says, "You feel constrained by society and what it expects of you. Society expects me not to burst into tears at the bus stop anymore." Kirsty and Nikki have some wise advice: "You don't need to move on... you just need to move forward."

Stuff and Possessions

We all have different feelings about stuff and things. If you're an on-the-move expat, for instance, you'll want to keep possessions to a minimum. Relationships with things evolve and change over time. The same happens at home. As people age, they want to pass on treasures and trinkets to their younger generations, and that could be you.

Anthropologist Eric Arnould and marketing scholar Linda Price studied the emotions and decisions surrounding the disposition of older Americans' cherished possessions at the end of life. They found that possessions have stories: where they came from, what they mean to the senior, what they hope they will mean to the recipient. The sharing of these stories when possessions are passed on gives reassurance to the elderly that intergenerational ties remain strong.

When you are in your 30s or 40s, you may think these gifts are like ancient relics that have no place in your home. But as the 50s approach, you'll develop a fresh appreciation of them and decide you actually like having that beautiful crystal or silverware on display - despite the burden of cleaning and dusting. These gifts have gained meaning for you, and there's a sense that stories have been passed on. I have many such items in my home, each one with a story.

If you are offered cherished possessions from home, I suggest you receive them with good grace. Even though they mean nothing to you now, they might in time.

Unequal decisions

When our parents pass and it's time to settle their affairs, we all hope the process will be straightforward and not inflamed by family angst. Sadly, this isn't always the case, even for the most stable of families. Emotions, regrets and hidden agendas can surface and affect sibling relationships.

Most parents start out dividing everything equally in their wills. But over time, and for many reasons (that are rightfully theirs), they may change their will, and things can end up being unequal as a result.

Unequal inheritances can be difficult. There are many reasons why people make the decisions they do. Often the best thing to do is graciously allow their wishes to be respected.

Reflection

Death at a distance is unequivocally hard. None of us know how we'll manage until the time comes. If it's two or three (or more) years down the track and you're still struggling to "move forward", as Nikki and Kirsty describe it, and if you've never considered counselling before, then this could be the time. Your parent or family member wouldn't want you to be 'stuck', and professionals can certainly help here. See the *Resources* section for global contacts.

I finish this chapter with two stories that impacted me. The first is an aspect of death at a distance that few of us have the privilege to experience, and the second talks of a legacy that made me reflect.

Flying Coffins

Dave is my hairdresser's husband and I have known him for over 20 years. He is quietly spoken and one of those chaps you'd call 'a good man'. Quite coincidentally, he has recently gained the less than welcomed title of distance grandparent, but that's not the focus here. Until his recent retirement, Dave had worked at Air New Zealand for decades. For much of that time he was a team leader in the Freight Department. And what does airline freight bring to mind? Sitting in New Zealand, I think of Pacific oysters winging their way to restaurants around the world and bold, spirited racehorses arriving home from the Melbourne Cup. And let's not forget all those adored pets relocating with their owners. But on a regular basis, air freight *also* includes the bodies of Distance Family.

As Dave once explained to me, the mood in the loading bay immediately changes when a coffin is expected. Waybills, customs forms and other documentation remain essential, but *people* take priority. Emotions are especially charged because relatives are on their way to take their loved one home.

Most cultures don't have an expectation that when family members die overseas, they will bring home the body. Many would *like* to, but it's not always realistic. But New Zealand's indigenous Māori place huge importance on returning the body to its land whenever possible. This enables the spirit of their dead, the spirit of their ancestors, to be set free in their homeland.

In a 2016 article, journalist Tom Hunt reported that in the previous year, 539 dead bodies arrived in New Zealand compared to just 199 that left for overseas (mainly tourists). That is well over one a day and nearly equivalent to the 544 passenger capacity of a double-decker Airbus A380.

It all starts with the family contacting a funeral director in the country of death, who arranges for the body to be embalmed locally and then air-shipped to New Zealand with the (complex) accompanying documentation. Most Māori body transfers come from Australia (a three-hour flight away), where there is a significant population of New Zealanders.

Out of respect, Air New Zealand prefers, where possible, to allocate the coffin its own unit load device (ULD): an aircraft freight container. The coffin doesn't share a space with general cargo. Once landed and processed, the coffin is wheeled to a dedicated viewing room.

A New Zealand funeral director then takes over, supporting the *whanau* (family) to welcome their loved one home. Dave told me that *whanau* may arrive dressed in their Sunday best or cruise to the airport on an imposing motorbike, clad in patched gang leather gear. Everyone is there for the same reason and they come together in harmony and union. The desire to let the deceased's spirit free is so urgent that occasionally a family member lifts the coffin lid to break the airtight enclosure before the rest of the family (and Dave) are quite ready. In a more recent conversation, Dave told me this act had stopped for various reasons.

Prayers are said and *waiatas* (traditional knowledge passed from one person to another) are sung. Family members hug and shed tears. There are facilities close by for the family to wash their hands upon departure. This ritual removes the sacredness of the interim death ceremony and allows the grieving family to return to the everyday world. (As a side note, you'll find a lonely water tap at most New Zealand cemeteries. Its primary purpose, once again, is for the family to wash their hands as they leave the cemetery.)

When formalities are over at the airport, the funeral director or the family then transport the deceased to the location of the *tangi* (funeral). This may mean a road trip of many hours.

Over the years Dave witnessed a countless number of these emotionally fuelled scenes. He was affected by every single one. "The one thing that was always apparent," he reflected, "was the sense of relief among families when the deceased arrived home."

Etchings in stone

On St Patrick's Day 2021, author and columnist Dan Barry published a moving article in *The New York Times*. When I read it, I thought of all the Distance Sons and Daughters in the world.

Dan's mother, like so many Irish people, left her homeland as a young woman and eked out a living on Long Island, U.S.A. In time, she was buried there. When Dan later travelled to Ireland and visited the church cemetery in the village where his relatives had lived, he noticed additions engraved into the gaps between the text on some headstones: deceased family members who lived far away got a small mention. He liked these 'bracketed' inserts and, in time, an accommodating stonemason, who emphasised the need for brevity, engraved a single line of text "near the lichen-mottled bottom" of the family headstone. It read: NOREEN BARRY 14 Nov 1937 - 18 Feb 1999 USA.

"I can't quite explain why I felt the need to add to the sacred text of an old Irish graveyard. Perhaps it had to do with wanting to return my mother to the ongoing conversation of her homeplace."

Dan Barry, *The New York Times*

I loved reading this article. In decades to come, when the Distance Sons and Daughters who are currently in their 30s, 40s or 50s have passed, will an unknown descendent visit a gravesite in what was at one time 'home' and leave a mark in the same way?

23. THE COVID EFFECT

"My own sense is that people, in a way, don't change that much emotionally but our lives are run by what happens around us... which we've felt very much with COVID. We've all had to adapt to a very different way of life."
Jenny Agutter, actress, Sister Julienne from *Call the Midwife*

There isn't a solitary geographically scattered family on the planet that hasn't been affected by COVID-19.

The pandemic constrained our ability to feed or 'top up' the part of our being that yearns for the occasional face-to-face, physical connection with our family and all that the home country means. The intensity of that yearning took some by surprise.

"The pandemic constrained our ability to feed or 'top up' the part of our being that yearns for the occasional face-to-face, physical connection with our family and all that the home country means. The intensity of that yearning took some by surprise."

Educator, researcher and leading family therapist Dr Pauline Boss, who penned the term 'ambiguous loss', has recently published a book discussing ambiguous loss and COVID-19. It's called *The Myth of Closure*. She talks of COVID-19 being like a light switch. One moment your loss (living with distance) was *voluntary*, and with the momentary click of a switch, it became *involuntary*.

As borders opened and closed sporadically around the world, not all Distance Families were in the same boat; some were able to reconnect more easily than others. But even for Distance Sons and Daughters who did connect, it was still 'a long time between drinks', as the saying goes. When this happens, you change, your Distance Family change and all the emotions around being a Distance Son or Daughter are further heightened.

"For us, it's not about wanting to jet set around the world for holidays: it's about wanting to cook a meal for my parents, sit down with a bottle of wine, and really find out how they are. It's about wanting to watch a film with my best friend and laugh until my ribs hurt. It's about living through some truly distressing times in history, and just wanting a hug from my mum."
George Fenwick, *Stuff*

In this chapter I address pandemic issues that, combined, have done several things:

- Affected Distance Sons and Daughters in a way they'll never forget
- Made all generations of Distance Families reassess much
- Changed the way we 'family'
- Left lasting damage for some

'We're Only 24 Hours Away From Home'

"In the global society new opportunities and changing systems may impact on the worldview that families adopt for their evolution of home.

These subjective processes may shape the level of attachment to a place... One cannot assume that the place you were born and raised is available to you for a home or that when you relocate you will have a stable status in which to create a home."
Professor Barbara Settles, *Journal of Comparative Family Studies*

"Every one of my toddlers' daycare friends has grandparents overseas. We all made this far-reaching life work, because we knew, if things went pear-shaped, we could be on a plane home within hours. That comfort has fritted away, like an air mattress deflating without warning."
Daisy Dumas, *The Guardian*

What makes Professor Settles' statement particularly insightful is that she published it in 2001 when globalisation was a trendy new term. Daisy Dumas wrote her article in 2020. Both tell us that life is full of uncertainties.

Before COVID-19, 'we're only 24 hours from home' was a cornerstone comfort cry for Distance Sons and Daughters. It was like a Monopoly 'get out of jail' card and a crucial and completely logical decision-making factor in moving abroad. When you felt homesick and needed a home 'fix', or someone at home needed you, a journey home was the solution. You had a plan. You'd find the funds somehow and you'd make it happen. Pre-COVID-19, flight travel was easy and fares were relatively cheap, and this gave reassurance to Distance Sons and Daughters who were concerned about homesickness and the need to 'be there'. It was a valid strategy and we all took it for granted.

The pandemic stole this plan. COVID-19 pulled the rug from under everyone's feet. Family members at home were upset, and worse still, some voiced the opinion that the forced separation was *your* fault. At the same time, there you were, struggling hopelessly with pandemic restrictions, uncertainty and risks.

As a side note for Distance Sons and Daughters, your distance parents and grandparents probably don't consider you to be 'only 24 hours away from home' in quite the same way you do. From conversations I've had, most are thinking that you have gone and that *maybe* (hopefully) you'll visit from time to time, and *maybe* they'll visit you. And even parents and grandparents who have previously travelled on last-minute 'being there' missions to visit you don't see themselves 'only 24 hours away' from their son or daughter. These subtle distinctions are important. They mean each generation of a Distance Family enters a pandemic with a different outlook.

Missed hatches, matches and despatches

During the pandemic, significant ceremonies and family rituals were missed. Grandchildren were born. I felt especially sad for first-time parents unable to hand over their new wee bundle to visiting first-time grandparents. You're only a first-time parent once and a first-time grandparent once. It's not the same a year or two down the track.

Weddings were celebrated with key family members missing from the top table. In our case, our son Robbie married in Chicago, and we had to be content with a virtual event.

There were many harrowing stories of families separated at times of crisis, illness and death.

Not to mention the thousands of families, like mine, who just wanted a hug.

This taught us that in-person family time is a precious commodity - in a way we hadn't considered before. We took for granted our ability to physically connect. Personally, I will never complain about jet lag again. It's a temporary consequence of our freedom.

Permanent (?) collateral damage

It is important to acknowledge the fallout for Distance Sons and Daughters who wanted - or sadly *needed* - to visit/return home during the pandemic and couldn't. When border restrictions and isolation rules were imposed, the regulations varied between 'home' countries, and they were ever-changing. There was a complete absence of certainty. As a New Zealander sitting in a country with some of the strictest pandemic regulations, I was only too aware of the agonising heartache from afar. Distance Sons and Daughters were locked out of their own country. For many, their relationship with home was tarnished and, in some cases, decimated. Will time be a healer? There are no guarantees, but I hope so.

Reconnecting

As visits become the new (albeit tentative) norm after pandemic restrictions, there are new things to consider.

Balancing risks

Travel has always come with risk, but post pandemic, we're all faced with new realities that require careful consideration. My own family is an example.

When New Zealand borders reopened after a three-year shutdown, our three overseas children were well and truly overdue to visit New Zealand and desperately wanted to. But when it came time to be *sensible* and put our 'risk analysis' hats on, we realised that for our daughter Lucy, visiting New Zealand with two co-parented sons, a business back home and the possibility of New Zealand's strict isolation rules kicking in again, the visit would have been fraught with risk. As Lucy said with great honesty, "We could end up isolating together for weeks, well past our booked return date. We'll be ready to kill each other." In the end we decided it would be easier (and less risky) for me and Clive to travel to America instead.

One of my key research findings in *Being a Distance Grandparent* is that change is a constant companion. As Clive and I were thinking about dusting off our suitcases, we were fortunate to be in a position where we could stand back, assess the situation and flip the programme. Flexibility, weighing up the pros and cons and having honest communication in both directions are powerful tools to help ride out any pandemic and adjust to whatever the new norm is.

Practical advice

Dr Kerry Byrne, founder of The Long Distance Grandparent Society, provides support to distance grandparents. In a conversation, I mentioned I was aware that many distance grandparents were nervous about reconnecting with their Distance Family again. She offered some wonderfully practical advice:

"After not seeing Grandpa or Grandma for a long time, children benefit from a bit of an emotional warm-up. As the parent, you can do this by working Grandma or Grandpa into everyday conversations - not in a forced way but in a more intentional way, especially leading up to a visit. Maybe Grandma is a person who perseveres against all odds or likes the same kind of ice cream as your child. Pointing this out helps to get children thinking about grandparents as more than a face on the video screen.

"There is often so much build-up about 'that moment' when they will see one another again. And sure, some children will gladly run into their grandparents' arms and give them the almighty long-awaited hug, but others take a while to warm up - whether it's to a grandparent they haven't seen for a while or a neighbour they saw yesterday!

"Having a homemade gift or a toy your child can give Grandma or Grandpa (even if you have to be the one to hand it over) can really break the ice and take the focus off the people and move it to the interaction.

"A Hot Wheels car for Grandpa and one for your child, alongside a roll of masking tape to create a car road together on the carpet, can go a long way towards easing everyone back into the importance of the time you will share together."

Certainties

"Over the last two years, the world has changed in ways that most of us could never have imagined. We are still living with the pandemic, but we are also experiencing a period of social, racial, economic and environmental reckoning that spans the world. Even if by some miracle, we were to all begin to return to a life without lockdown tomorrow, the aftershocks of all these realities combined will be felt for a long time to come."

'FIGT 2022', Families in Global Transition

In a recent email to members of the Association of Social Anthropologists of Aotearoa/New Zealand, one of my lecturers from Massey University, Dr Graeme MacRae, said this: "As anthropologists, we know better than most that 'normal' isn't necessarily normal and 'other worlds are possible'." Dr MacRae also suggested that anthropologists should take responsibility to contribute to this debate. As a fledging anthropologist, I will do my best.

Weighing up Distance Familying pre-COVID-19 and post-COVID-19, there are *some* certainties about whatever our new normal will be:

- COVID-19 will forever affect us. Our experiences will impact the way we conduct our lives in the future.
- We will never take for granted the ability to fly around the world and physically connect with families.
- Non-changeable, non-refundable airfares have little appeal and will become a dinosaur of the past.
- COVID-19 has been a viral war, and wartime experiences build bonds.
- Western globalisation and migration are no longer dominated only by pull factors. Push factors are now evident.
- Western globalisation and its ease of mobility has lost its sparkle for some. Foreign career assignments that involve migration and work overseas will become less common in the future.
- Distance Families with a mixture of vaxxed and unvaxxed family members may cope with a layer of hesitancy regarding contact - in a way they've never considered or experienced before. Even when governments decree that citizens can travel, travel insurance companies will have the last say and may not provide fully comprehensive medical cover (including for pandemics).

Reflection

Living abroad may have lost some of its sparkle, but it is still thrilling to have international connections within family generations. I remain grateful for our globalisation-infused family, and I know with certainty that the pandemic brought us closer together. I hope it did for you.

To Distance Sons and Daughters, don't give up on the dream of experiencing diverse cultures, being challenged in new environments and taking your family on the biggest adventure of their life.

To all generations of Distance Families:

With knowledge comes understanding

With understanding comes empathy

And empathy is a good thing for Distance Families

RESOURCES

These resources are regularly updated at:
www.DistanceFamilies.com/resources

The Distance Family Book Series

If this book has piqued your interest in Distance Families - don't stop. Here are my other two titles:

Being a Distance Grandparent - a Book for ALL Generations

Being a Distance Grandchild - a Book for ALL Generations

Being a Distance Son or Daughter is just one-third of the Distance Families story. If your goal is to increase your understanding and empathy for the other generations in your family, these books are for you.

Visit www.DistanceFamilies.com for publication details and where to purchase.

Books

***The 5 Love Languages* by Gary Chapman**
Northfield Publishing, 1992

Chapman has written an extensive range of books focusing on *The 5 Love Languages.* Be sure to check out all his titles. Opportunities to show your love to your Distance Family are all too brief. Once you understand the love language principles, it will help you appreciate how *you* like to be loved but more importantly how each member of your family likes to be loved. For example, don't waste money sending endless presents to a person who isn't a 'Gifts love language' person. To a certain degree, presents are wasted on them. In contrast, be sure to give a 'Quality Time love language' family member your undivided attention, without distractions, whenever you call. These are easy habits to embrace and incredibly effective. This is one of the most powerful, incredibly useful books I have ever read.

It's All About Relationships by Karen L. Rancourt
Family Links Press, 2019

Karen's relationship book is the culmination of decades of work, research and book writing supporting parents/grandparents and their adult children (and vice versa). What I like most is that each time Karen presents a tricky issue scenario within a family or at work, she first explains that there are many ways to deal with it (and all can be right), but she *also* gives you the likely outcome of each option. That is powerful and it takes years of experience learning how people tick to be able to make these predictions. Dr Rancourt wrote the foreword for this book.

Third Culture Kids by David C. Pollock, Ruth E. Van Reken and Michael V. Pollock
Nicholas Brealey Publishing, 3rd edition, 2017

If you have a strong interest in globally mobile families, this is the 'TCK Bible': foundational teachings of growing up multiculturally.

Fault Lines: Fractured Families and How to Mend Them by Karl Pillemer
Avery/Penguin Random House, 2020

If you have estrangement in your family, I can't recommend this book highly enough. Distance Family estrangement could be as basic as a Distance Son or Daughter (or in-law) preferring not to be present during video call catch-ups. It's tough. This book will help give you some answers.

Stop Walking on Eggshells **by Paul T.T. Mason and Randi Kreger**
New Harbinger Publications, Inc, 2nd edition, 2010

If a member of your family continuously dwells on the past, is controlling and appears to have issues with everyone and everything (could even be described as 'toxic'), this book will not necessarily solve the problem but will put this person's behaviour into perspective.

Beyond Your Bubble **by Tania Israel**
American Psychological Association, 2020

If political polarisation exists in your family *and* you want to do something about it, this is a wonderful tool. It is an easy-read handbook with a paint-by-numbers method of finding common ground and understanding, not necessarily changing, others' views.

Rules of Estrangement **by Joshua Coleman**
Sheldon Press, 2021

Joshua Coleman understands you as he has 'been there'. Estrangement can be reversed, and he offers solutions. A must-read. "*I've found that understanding the social causes of estrangement helps parents feel less alone, less guilty, and less ashamed.*" (Joshua Coleman)

Parental Guidance: Long Distance Care for Aging Parents **by Ana McGinley, 2016**

This is a dynamo book full of terrific advice. Ana has a medical background. I'd recommend owning the e-book version rather than the paperback so it's always easily accessible. There's excellent advice covering medical issues, legal/financial issues and dealing with hospitals and authorities in person and from afar.

Your D.I.Y. Move Guide to Australia **by Robyn Vogels and Hendrika Jooste**
Your Move Guide, 2020

A filled-to-the-brim book full of practical advice for any destination, especially Australia.

A Parent's Guide to Raising Kids Overseas **by Jeff Devens, PhD, 2018**

If you're an expat parent, especially if your children are attending an international school, you'll find answers to many questions - even to the ones you might be a tad hesitant to ask.

Holding the Fort Abroad **by Rhoda Bangerter**
Summertime Publishing, 2021

If one or other of you travel extensively with your job, this is a must-own.

Expat Partner **by Carine Bormans and Marie Geukens**
LannooCampus, 2020

How to navigate being an expat partner and making the most of each posting.

Whose Career - Yours, Mine or Ours? **by Yvonne Quahe**
Summertime Publishing, 2021

Addressing the dual career dilemma with care.

Websites

Distance Families: www.DistanceFamilies.com. The website for this book series

Families in Global Transition:(www.figt.org. A globally mobile forum for individuals, families and those working with them

Social Media

Distance Families: www.facebook.com/DistanceFamilies. The Facebook page for this book series

Facebook: www.facebook.com/groups/distancegrandparent. A private Facebook group for Distance Grandparents (connected to DistanceFamilies.com).

Instagram: @helenellis.author

Professional Services

Families in Global Transition. The Counseling and Coaching Affiliate. A professional subgroup in the FIGT community. www.figt.org/counseling-coaching-affiliate.

For additional professional and counselling services, please visit: www.DistanceFamilies.com/resources

BIBLIOGRAPHY

ABOUT THIS BOOK

Comer, Diane (2019), *The Braided River: Migration and the Personal Essay*, Otago University Press: Dunedin, N.Z.

Eriksen, Thomas Hylland (2010), 'The challenges of anthropology', *International Journal of Pluralism and Education*, Vol. 1, iss. 3, pp. 194-202

Gibbons, Ruth (2018), 'The Life of the Anthropologist: Improvised and Living Between', Conference Programme, ASSANZ 2018

Koutonin, Mawuna Remarque (2015), 'Why are white people expats when the rest of us are immigrants?', *The Guardian*,

https://www.theguardian.com/global-development-professionals-network/2015/mar/13/white-people-expats-immigrants-migration

Ottimofiore, Mariam Navaid (2019), *This Messy Mobile Life*, Springtime Books: United Kingdom

Rancourt, Dr. Karen L. (2019), *It's All About Relationships: New Ways to Make Them Healthy and Fulfilling, at Home and at Work*, Family Links Press: U.S.A.

Tett, Gillian (2021), *Anthro Vision: How Anthropology Can Explain Business and Life*, Penguin: London, U.K.

Wildfire, Jessica (2017), 'You don't have to love your family', *Medium*, https://medium.com/the-hit-job/you-dont-have-to-love-your-family-fcf66b5a151d

1. UNDERSTANDING DISTANCE PARENTS AND DISTANCE GRANDPARENTS

Baggini, Julian (2018), *How the World Thinks: A Global History of Philosophy*, Granta Books: London, U.K.

2. UNPACKING DISTANCE SONS AND DAUGHTERS

Bangerter, Rhoda (2021), Correspondence. *Holding the Fort Abroad*, Summertime Publishing: United Kingdom

Halabi, Faisal (2020), 'Opinion: We are at war with Covid-19, and ourselves', *Radio New Zealand*, https://www.rnz.co.nz/news/on-the-inside/412738/opinion-we-are-at-war-with-covid-19-and-ourselves

Hallett Mobbs, Carole (2021), *ExpatChild*, LinkedIn post, https://www.linkedin.com/posts/carolehallettmobbs_i-want-to-move-overseas-how-to-do-that-and-activity-6851418252015353856-x1Ds/

Scott, Amy (2021), Conversation. *Nomadtopia*, www.nomadtopia.com

3. UNPACKING EMOTIONS

Bangerter, Rhoda (2021), Correspondence. *Holding the Fort Abroad*, Summertime Publishing: United Kingdom

Baldassar, Loretta (2001), *Visits Home: Migration Experiences Between Italy and Australia*, Melbourne University Press: Melbourne, Australia

Bille, Mikkel, Hastrup, Frida & Sørensen, Tim Flohr (Eds.) (2010), *An Anthropology of Absence: Materializations of Transcendence and Loss*, Springer Science & Business Media: NY.

Boccagni, Paolo & Baldassar, Loretta (2015), 'Emotions on the move: Mapping the emergent field of emotion and migration', *Emotion, Space and Society*, Vol. 16, pp. 73-80

Boss, Pauline (2016), 'The Context and Process of Theory Development: The Story of Ambiguous Loss', *Journal of Family Theory & Review*, Vol. 8, iss. 3, pp. 269-286

Connidis, Ingrid Arnet (2015), 'Exploring Ambivalence in Family Ties: Progress and Prospects', *Journal of Marriage and Family*, Vol. 77, pp. 77-95

Crossman, Tanya (2018), 'Expat guilt: being far from family', *Misunderstood*, https://misunderstood-book.com/2018/09/20/expat-guilt-being-far-from-family

Gottlieb, Lori (2021), LinkedIn post, https://www.linkedin.com/posts/lori-gottlieb-9b18013_deartherapists-podcast-activity-6850478567701270528-A_0r/

Hallett Mobbs, Carole (2016), 'Expat guilt', *ExpatChild*, https://expatchild.com/expat-guilt

Harris, Jodi (2018), 'Why Gratitude is the Best Answer for Difficult Expat Emotions', *World Tree Coaching*, https://www.worldtreecoaching.com/why-gratitude-is-the-best-answer-for-difficult-expat-emotions

Matthews, Leigh (2021), 'Restless, Rootlessness & Resilience' in Carrie Frais (Ed.), *#LivingTheDream*, Springtime Books: United Kingdom

Meza-Rapp, Melissa, (2019), 'The Perpetual Foreigner', in Lorna Jane Harvey (Ed.), *Somewhere: Women's Stories of Migration*, Beatnik Publishing: Auckland, N.Z.

Ottimofiore, Mariam Navaid (2019), *This Messy Mobile Life*, Springtime Books: United Kingdom

Skrbiš, Zlatko (2008), 'Transnational Families: Theorising Migration, Emotions and Belonging', *Journal of Intercultural Studies*, Vol. 29, iss. 3, pp. 231-246

Solheim, Catherine A. & Ballard, Jaimie (2016), 'Ambiguous Loss Due to Separation in Voluntary Transnational Families', *Journal of Family Theory & Review*, Vol. 8, pp. 341359

5. BEFORE YOU LEAVE

Bormans, Carine & Geukens, Marie (2020), *Expat Partner: Staying Active & Finding Work*, Lannoo Campus: Leuven, Belgium

Fesenmyer, Leslie E. (2014), 'Transnational Families', in Keith, M. & Anderson, B. (Eds.), *Migration: The COMPAS Anthology*, COMPAS: Oxford, U.K.

Jones, Jerry (2019), 'When your last goodbye was your last goodbye: Processing death and life abroad', *the culture blend*, http://www.theculturеblend.com/when-your-last-goodbye-was-your-last-goodbye-processing-death-and-life-abroad

Marchette-Mercer, Maria (n.d.), 'Experience', LinkedIn post, https://www.linkedin.com/in/maria-marchetti-mercer/?originalSubdomain=za

Marchette-Mercer, Maria (2017), "The Screen Has Such Sharp Edges to Hug": The Relational Consequences of Emigration in Transnational South African Emigrant Families, *Transnational Social Review*, Vol. 7, Iss. 1, pp. 73-89

TeamViewer (2022) https://www.teamviewer.com

Vogels, Robyn & Jooste, Hendrika (2020), *Your D.I.Y. Move Guide to Australia*, Your Move Guide: Melbourne, Australia

6. SETTLING IN

Bangerter, Rhoda (2021), *Holding the Fort Abroad*, Summertime Publishing: United Kingdom

Devens, Jeff (2018), *A Parent's Guide to Raising Kids Overseas*, CreateSpace Independent Publishing Platform

Fesenmyer, Leslie E. (2014), 'Transnational Families', in Keith, M. & Anderson, B. (Eds.), *Migration: The COMPAS Anthology*, COMPAS: Oxford, U.K.

Spoonley, Paul (2020), *The New New Zealand*, Massey University Press: Auckland, N.Z.

Winnard, Natasha (2021), Conversation https://www.natashawinnard.com

7. NAVIGATING WORK

Bormans, Carine & Geukens, Marie (2020), *Expat Partner: Staying Active & Finding Work*, Lannoo Campus: Leuven, Belgium

Coggiola, Sara (2021), Correspondence. Instagram@sarabetweencultures, https://www.instagram.com/sarabetweencultures

Marcela (2019), cited in Comer, Diane, *The Braided River: Migration and the Personal Essay*, Otago University Press: Dunedin, N.Z.

Obama, Michelle (July 2020), 'President Barack Obama', *The Michelle Obama Podcast*, https://open.spotify.com/episode/5JzuNYOm8p6u5WzU9VBWid

Quahe, Yvonne (2021), *Whose Career - Yours, Mine or Ours?*, Springtime Books: United Kingdom

Wright, Molly (2021), 'How every child can thrive by five', *TED Talks*, https://www.ted.com/talks/molly_wright_how_every_child_can_thrive_by_five

8. IDENTITY AND THE MEANING OF HOME

Comer, Diane (2019), *The Braided River: Migration and the Personal Essay*, Otago University Press: Dunedin, N.Z.

Kisvardai, Marianna (2020), 'Where is Home for an Expat?', *The Expat Magazine*, https://www.thexpatmagazine.com/blog/2020-06-14-where-is-home-for-an-expat

9. CULTURE AND LANGUAGE

Adam, Hajo et al. (2018), 'How Living Abroad Helps You Develop a Clearer Sense of Self', *Harvard Business*

Review, https://hbr.org/2018/05/how-living-abroad-helps-you-develop-a-clearer-sense-of-self

Baggini, Julian (2018), *How the World Thinks: A Global History of Philosophy*, Granta Books: London, U.K.

Cohen, Melisa (2021), Conversation. www.pureresults.co.nz

Comer, Diane (2019), *The Braided River: Migration and the Personal Essay*, Otago University Press: Dunedin, N.Z.

Harvey, Lorna Jane (2019), *Somewhere: Women's Stories of Migration,* Beatnik: Auckland, N.Z.

Jhanb, Sneha (2020), 'Incorporating Grandparents' Parenting Technique', in Singh, Aditi Wardhan (curator), *Raising the Global Mindset*, Raising World Children LLC

Kutor, Senanu K, Railenanu, Alexandru & Simandan, Dragos (2021), 'International migration, cross-cultural interaction, and the development of personal wisdom', *Migration Studies*, Vol. 9, iss. 3, pp. 490-513

Lanzerotta, Shannon (2020), 'Effect of Language Learning on Growth', in Singh, Aditi Wardhan (curator), *Raising the Global Mindset*, Raising World Children LLC

Limacher-Riebold, Ute (2022), Online workshop, 'How our language use changes during our international life', FIGT Australia and New Zealand

Limacher-Riebold, Ute & Martin, Karin (27 Oct 2021), 'How To Raise Multilingual Children', Online seminar, Families in Global Transition: Australia, New Zealand Affiliate (FIGT ANZA)

McCarthy, Patti (2016), *Cultural Chemistry: Simple Strategies for Bridging Cultural Gaps*, Cultural Chemistry

Nesteruk, Olena & Marks, Loren (2009), 'Grandparents Across the Ocean: Eastern European Immigrants' Struggle to Maintain Intergenerational Relationships', *Journal of Comparative Family Studies*, Vol. 40, iss. 1, pp. 77-95

O'Brien, Josephine (2020), 'Multicultural Family Problems', in Singh, Aditi Wardhan (curator), *Raising the Global Mindset*, Raising World Children LLC

Ottimofiore, Mariam Navaid (2019), *This Messy Mobile Life*, Springtime Books: United Kingdom

Quahe, Yvonne (2021), *Whose Career - Yours, Mine or Ours?*, Springtime Books: United Kingdom

Smurthwaite, Dave (2021), 'Why Americans Die on Donuts while the French Thrive on Pastries', *Medium*, https://medium.com/mindtrip/why-americans-die-on-donuts-while-the-french-thrive-on-pastries-b98f251c0222

10. NAVIGATING THE DISTANCE

Baldassar, Loretta (2007), 'Transnational Families and the Provision of Moral and Emotional Support: The Relationship between Truth and Distance', *Identities: Global Studies in Culture and Power*, Vol. 14, iss. 4, pp. 385-409

Byrne, Dr. Kerry (2021), 'The #1 Secret of Long-Distance Grandparenting', *GaGa Sisterhood*, https://www.gagasisterhood.com/2021/the-1-secret-of-long-distance-grandparenting

Chapman, Gary (1992), *The 5 Love Languages*, Northfield Publishing: Northfield, MA.

Eriksen, Dr. Karen (2020), Email correspondence.

Golant, Stephen M. (2017), 'Will older people use smart technologies designed to improve the quality of their lives?', *Atlas of Science*, https://atlasofscience.org/will-older-people-use-smart-technologies-designed-to-improve-the-quality-of-their-lives

Hartnett, Paddy (2021), Email conversation. www.paddyhartnett.com

Kalish, Nancy (2010), 'Over The River & Through The Woods: Long Distance Grandparenting', *Psychology*

Today, https://www.psychologytoday.com/us/blog/sticky-bonds/201006/over-the-river-through-the-woods-long-distance-grandparenting

McGinley, Ana (2016), *Parental Guidance: Long Distance Care for Aging Parents*, CreateSpace Independent Publishing Platform

Neustaedter, Carman, Harrison, Steve & Sellen, Abigail (2013), *Connecting Families*,

Springer-Verlag: London, U.K.

Rancourt, Dr. Karen L. (2019), *It's All About Relationships: New Ways to Make Them Healthy and Fulfilling, at Home and at Work*, Family Links Press: U.S.A.

11. DISTANCE FAMILY RELATIONSHIPS: IN GENERAL

Baldassar, Loretta (2007) 'Transnational Families and the Provision of Moral and Emotional Support: the Relationship Between Truth and Distance', *Identities: Global Studies in Culture and Power*, Vol. 14, iss. 4, pp. 385-409

Bloomfield, Keri (2021), Email conversation. https://www.keribloomfield.com

Crossman, Tanya (2021), Email conversation. https://www.tanyacrossman.com

Finlayson, Kris (2022), Email correspondence. https://www.linkedin.com/in/krisfinlayson

Mackenzie, Sarah (2018), *The Read-Aloud Family*, Zondervan: Grand Rapids, MI.

Majuri, Charles E. (2011), 'Grandparent Gardening Gifts: The Enduring Gifts Grandparents Can Offer Their Grandchildren', *Journal of Therapeutic Horticulture*, Vol. 11, iss. 1, pp. 41-43

Pahl, Raymond & Pevalin, David J (2005), 'Between family and friends: A longitudinal study of friendship choice', *British Journal of Sociology*, Vol. 56, iss. 3, pp. 433-450

Pollock, D.C., Van Reken, R.E. & Pollock, M. (2017), *Third Culture Kids*, 3rd ed., Nicholas Brealey Publishing: London, U.K.

Rancourt, Dr. Karen L (2019), *It's All About Relationships: New Ways to Make Them Healthy and Fulfilling, at Home and at Work*, Family Links Press: U.S.A.

Rolheiser, Ronald (14 June 2020), 'Faithful friendship', *NZ Catholic*

Romanes, Bridget (2020), 'Lessons From a Pandemic: Evolving Relocation Support in New Zealand', *Thriving Abroad*,

https://www.thrivingabroad.com/lessons-from-a-pandemic-evolving-relocation-support-in-new-zealand

Skrbiš, Zlatko (2008), 'Transnational Families: Theorising Migration, Emotions and Belonging', *Journal of Intercultural Studies*, Vol. 29, iss. 3, pp. 231-246

12. DISTANCE FAMILY RELATIONSHIPS: PARENTS AND GRANDPARENTS

Burns, Jim (2019), *Doing Life with Your Adult Children: Keep Your Mouth Shut and the Welcome Mat Out*, Zondervan: Grand Rapids, MI.

Coleman, Joshua (2021), *Rules of Estrangement: Why Adult Children Cut Ties and How to Heal the Conflict*, Sheldon Press: United Kingdom

Dempsey, Deborah & Lindsay, Jo (2014), *Families, relationships and intimate life*, Oxford University Press: South Melbourne, Australia

Gottlieb, Lori (2020), 'Dear Therapist: My Daughter Doesn't Care That I Want Her to Live Close to Home', *The Atlantic*, https://www.theatlantic.com/family/archive/2020/06/dear-therapist-my-daughter-lives-too-far-me/612412

Gransnet (2013), *The New Granny's Survival Guide*, Penguin: London, U.K.

Hax, Carolyn (2022), 'Carolyn Hax: In-laws reject their grandchild's combined last name', *The Washington Post*, https://www.washingtonpost.com/advice/2022/01/21/carolyn-hax-in-laws-reject-combined-last-name

Lagarrigue, Karina (2021), Email conversation. https://www.lagarrigue-psicologia.com

Pillemer, Karl (2020), *Fault Lines*, Avery, Penguin Random House: New York, NY.

Tanner, Victoria (2020), 'How to tackle tough times when you're missing "home"'. https://www.victoriatanner.com/articles/missing-home

Tuttle Carol and Tuttle Brown, Anne (n.d.), 'What Is the Healthy Role of a Grandparent?', *Live Your Truth*, https://cw.liveyourtruth.com/what-is-the-healthy-role-of-a-grandparent

13. DISTANCE FAMILY RELATIONSHIPS: SIBLINGS AND OTHERS

Ottimofiore, Mariam Navaid (2019), *This Messy Mobile Life*, Springtime Books: United Kingdom

Pillemer, Karl (2020), *Fault Lines*, Avery, Penguin Random House: New York, NY.

14. DISTANCE FAMILY RELATIONSHIPS: UPSET AND MAYHEM

Agrawal, Hans R., Gunderson, John, Holmes Bjarne M. & Lyons-Ruth, Karlen (2004), 'Attachment Studies with Borderline Patients: A Review', *Harvard Review Of Psychiatry*, Vol. 12, iss. 2, pp. 94-104

Berry, Keith & Adams, Tony E. (2016), 'Family Bullies', *Journal of Family Communication*, Vol. 16, iss. 1, pp. 51-63

Coleman, Joshua (2021), *Rules of Estrangement: Why Adult Children Cut Ties and How to Heal the Conflict*, Sheldon Press: United Kingdom

Devens, Jeff (2018), *A Parent's Guide to Raising Kids Overseas*, CreateSpace Independent Publishing Platform

Fraley, R. Chris (2018), 'Adult Attachment Theory and Research', Department of Psychology, University of Illinois, http://labs.psychology.illinois.edu/~rcfraley/attachment.htm

Gottlieb, Lori (2020), 'Dear Therapist: I Can't Stand My Dad's New Wife', *The Atlantic*, https://www.theatlantic.com/family/archive/2020/06/i-cant-stand-my-dads-new-wife/613588/

Hax, Carolyn (2012), 'Carolyn Hax: Keeping peace with the in-laws: disapproving of son's girlfriend', *Washington Post*,

https://www.washingtonpost.com/lifestyle/style/carolyn-hax-keeping-peace-with-the-in-laws-disapproving-of-sons-girlfriend/2012/06/12/gJQAX0IIYV_story.html

Israel, Tania (2020), *Beyond You Bubble: How to Connect Across the Political Divide, Skills and Strategies for Conversations That Work*, American Psychological Association: Washington D.C.

Mason, Paul T. & Kreger, Randi (2020), *Stop Walking on Eggshells: Taking Your Life Back When Someone You Care About Has Borderline Personality Disorder*, 3rd ed., New Harbinger Publications: Oakland, C.A.

Pillemer, Karl (2020), *Fault Lines*, Avery, Penguin Random House: New York, NY.

Rancourt, Dr. Karen L. (2019), *It's All About Relationships: New Ways to Make Them Healthy and Fulfilling, at Home and at Work*, Family Links Press: U.S.A.

Rogers, Emily (2020), '3 Steps to Maintain Calm', *Expat Parenting Abroad*, https://www.expatparentingabroad.com/blog/3-steps-to-maintain-calm

Singh, Inder (2021), 'Killing it with Kindness: How Respect Can Change the COVID Game', *Medium*, https://inder-singh.medium.com/killing-it-with-kindness-how-respect-can-change-the-covid-game-d63342137c1d

Turner, Toko-pa (2017), *Belonging: Remembering Ourselves Home*, Her Own Room Press: Salt Spring, BC, Canada

Van der Kolk, Bessel (2015), *The Body Keeps the Score*, Penguin Books: New York, NY.

Wassermann, Selma (2001), *The Long Distance Grandmother*, Hartley & Marks Publishers Inc: Vancouver, Canada

Zhou, Youyou (2018), 'The data show that how we connect with romantic partners changes as we age', *Quartz*, https://qz.com/1206940/attachment-style-changes-with-age/

15. BEING A DISTANCE CHILD (OF)

Anderson, Dr. Laura (2021), Email communication. www.drlauraanderson.com

Brew, Cath (2021), Email correspondence. www.drawntoastory.com

InterNations (n.d.), 'LGBT Expats and Their Partners', *InterNations*,

https://www.internations.org/guide/global/non-traditional-expat-partners-15292/lgbt-expats-and-their-partners-2

16. VISITS: IN GENERAL

Jaeger, Dr. Sonia (2021), Email communication. www.sonia-jaeger.com

Janta, H, Cohen, S.A. & Williams, A.M. (2015), 'Rethinking Visiting Friends and Relatives Mobilities', *Population, Space and Place*, Vol. 21, pp. 585-598

Morrow-Kondos, Diane (2021), 'A Grandmother's Love and Limits: A Letter to My Mom',

TulsaKids, https://www.tulsakids.com/a-grandmothers-love-and-limits/

17. VISITS: YOU GO HOME

Carnegie, Dale (1981), *How to Win Friends and Influence People*, Simon & Schuster: New York, NY.

Challa, Madhu (2020), 'Struggles of Expat Life', in Singh, Aditi Wardhan (curator), *Raising the Global Mindset*, Raising World Children LLC

Isay, Jane (2019), *Unconditional Love: A Guide to Navigating the Joys and Challenges of Being a Grandparent Today*, HarperCollins Publishing: New York, NY.

Ottimofiore, Mariam Navaid (2019), *This Messy Mobile Life*, Springtime Books: United Kingdom

Parfitt, Jo (2012), 'The Horror of Holidays', in Jo Parfitt (Ed.), *Forced to Fly*, Summertime Publishing: United Kingdom

Peters, Cheryl L, Hooker, Karen & Zvonkovic, Anisa, M (2006), 'Older Parents' Perceptions of Ambivalence in Relationships With Their Children', *Family Relations*, Vol. 55, pp. 538-551

Schneider-Bean, Sundae (2015), 'What gets stirred up when expats visit home', https://www.sundaebean.com/2015/07/28/expat-traps-when-visiting-home

Settles, Barbara H. (2001), 'Being at Home in a Global Society: A Model for Families' Mobility and Immigration Decisions', *Journal of Comparative Family Studies*, Vol. 32, iss. 4, pp. 627-645

Vogels, Robyn & Jooste, Hendrika (2020), *Your D.I.Y. Move Guide to Australia*, Your Move Guide: Melbourne, Australia

18. VISITS: THEY COME TO YOU

Comer, Diane (2019), *The Braided River: Migration and the Personal Essay*, Otago University Press: Dunedin, N.Z.

Devens, Jeff (2018), *A Parent's Guide to Raising Kids Overseas*, CreateSpace Independent Publishing Platform

Gosling, Peter (2012), 'Another Suitcase Another Long Haul', in Jo Parfitt (Ed.), *Forced to Fly*, Summertime Publishing: United Kingdom

Taylor, Jane (2002), 'Finding out what is important', in Dench (Ed.), *Grandmothers*, Transaction Publishers: London, U.K.

19. REPATRIATION IS A BIGGIE

Anderson, Margot (2021), *Boomeranging: Expat to Repat*, https://www.insyncnetworkgroup.com/podcast/

Gardner, Marilyn (2021), 'Repatriation or Re-entry', FIGT 2021 Virtual Conference

Kumar, Sindhuja (2020), 'Moving Back to Native Country', in Singh, Aditi Wardhan (curator), *Raising the Global Mindset*, Raising World Children LLC

Parks, Melissa Dr. (2021), Conversation. www.intentionalexpat.com

Seidel, Anna (2020), 'Repatriation Part 2: Taxiing in, the First Few Months', https://globalmobilitytrainer.com/repatriation-part-2-taxiing-in/

Stevenson, Tom (2019), 'The Hardest Part of Living Abroad Nobody Talks About', *Medium*, https://tom-stevenson.medium.com/the-hardest-part-of-living-abroad-nobody-talks-about-e7ed0fc07cf1

Storti, Craig (2003), *The Art of Coming Home*, Intercultural Press: Boston, M.A.

Twisk, Esther (2021), 'Reverse culture shock: Why returning home can be hard', *Expat Magazine*, https://www.

expat.com/en/expat-mag/5843-how-hard-is-the-reverse-culture-shock-for-long-term-expats.html

20. FINANCIAL COMINGS AND GOINGS

Britt, Sonya L. (2016), 'The Intergenerational Transference of Money Attitudes and Behaviors', *The Journal of Consumer Affairs*, Vol. 50, iss. 3, pp. 539-556

Coleman, Joshua (2021), *Rules of Estrangement: Why Adult Children Cut Ties and How to Heal the Conflict*, Sheldon Press: United Kingdom

McGinley, Ana (2016), *Parental Guidance: Long Distance Care for Aging Parents*, CreateSpace Independent Publishing Platform

21. DECLINE AND CARING AT A DISTANCE

Baldassar, L., Vellekoop Baldock, C. & Wilding, R. (2007), *Families Caring Across Borders*, Palgrave Macmillan: Basingstoke, U.K.

Baldassar, Loretta (2007), 'Transnational Families and the Provision of Moral and Emotional Support: the Relationship Between Truth and Distance', *Identities: Global Studies in Culture and Power*, Vol. 14, iss. 4, pp. 385-409

Bangerter, Rhoda (2021), *Holding the Fort Abroad*, Summertime Books, U.K.

Bangerter, Rhoda (2021), Email conversation.

Brooks, David (2020), 'Nine Nonobvious Ways to Have Deeper Conversations', *The New York Times*, https://www.nytimes.com/2020/11/19/opinion/nine-nonobvious-ways-to-have-deeper-conversations.html

Carstensen, Laura (2021), 'Socioemotional Selectivity Theory: The Role of Perceived Endings in Human Motivation', *The Gerontologist*, Vol. 16, iss. 8, pp. 1188-1196

Dastagir, Alia E. (2021), 'Furious at your parents for aging? You're not alone', *USA TODAY*, https://amp-usatoday-com.cdn.ampproject.org/c/s/amp.usatoday.com/amp/7901360002

Farrelly, Colin (2021), 'The COVID-19 Pandemic, Biogerontology, and the Ageing of Humanity', *The Gerontological Society of America*, Vol. 76, iss. 8, pp. 92-96

Fong, Mei (2016), *One Child*, Oneworld Publications: London, U.K.

Gardner, Marilyn R. (2014), 'The Autumn of My Parents', *Communicating Across Boundaries*, https://communicatingacrossboundariesblog.com/2014/10/24/the-autumn-of-my-parents

Golant, Stephen M. (2017), 'Will older people use smart technologies designed to improve the quality of their lives?', *Atlas of Science*,

https://atlasofscience.org/will-older-people-use-smart-technologies-designed-to-improve-the-quality-of-their-lives/

Katarzyna (2019), 'Far Away And Growing Old', *Medium*, https://medium.com/@katarzyniko/far-away-and-growing-old-b3b4ad66ef8b

McGinley, Ana (2016), *Parental Guidance: Long Distance Care for Aging Parents*, CreateSpace Independent Publishing Platform

Pillemer, Karl (2020), *Fault Lines*, Avery, Penguin Random House: New York, NY.

Porto, Carolina (2022). Email communication. https://www.carolinaporto.net

Rolheiser, Ronald (2020), 'Deeper things under the surface', *NZ Catholic*

Scott, Amy (2021), 'Long-distance family dynamics with Helen Ellis', podcast, *Nomadtopia*, https://www.nomadtopia.com/helenellis

Williams, Susan (n.d.), 'The Shift From Helicopter Parents to Helicopter Caregivers', *Booming*

Encore, https://boomingencore.com/en/article/shift-helicopter-parents-helicopter-caregivers

22. DEATH AT A DISTANCE AND SETTLING AFFAIRS

Arnould, Eric J. and Price Linda L. (2009), 'Cherished Possession', *Anthropology News*, Vol. 40, iss. 2, pp. 17-18

Barry, Dan (2021), 'I Brought My Mother Home to Ireland', *The New York Times*, https://www.nytimes.com/2021/03/17/opinion/ireland-family-cemetery.html

Gidley, Apple (2011), 'Global grandparenting is great but it can't beat a neck nuzzle'.

The Telegraph, https://www.telegraph.co.uk/expat/expatlife/8831091/Global-grandparenting-is-great-but-it-cant-beat-a-good-old-fashioned-neck-nuzzle.html

Goodison, David (2021), Conversation.

Hunt, Tom (2016), 'Hundreds of corpses enter NZ each year', *Stuff*, https://www.stuff.co.nz/national/81703396/hundreds-of-corpses-enter-nz-each-year

Neustaedter, Carman, Harrison, Steve & Sellen, Abigail (2013), *Connecting Families*,

Springer-Verlag: London, U.K.

McGinley, Ana (2016), *Parental Guidance: Long Distance Care for Aging Parents*, CreateSpace Independent Publishing Platform

Pillemer, Karl (2020), *Fault Lines*, Avery, Penguin Random House: New York, NY.

Rice, Kirsty & Moffitt, Nikki (2021), 'Did she just say her clivia had flowered?', podcast, *Two Fat Expats*, https://podcastaddict.com/episode/128172442

Vogels, Robyn (2021), Conversation. https://personnelrelocations.com.au/about

23. THE COVID EFFECT

Agutter, Jenny (2021), 'Celebrating 10 Years of Call the Midwife', Royal Television Society,https://www.youtube.com/watch?v=yzDV3TOFI7O

Byrne, Dr. Kerry (2021), Conversation. www.thelongdistancegrandparent.com

Boss, Pauline (2021), *The Myth of Closure: Ambiguous Loss in a Time of Pandemic and Change*, W.W. Norton & Co.: New York, NY.

Dumas, Daisy (2020), 'With borders closed, our lifelines to family overseas have been cut. The isolation is suffocating', *The Guardian*, https://www.theguardian.com/commentisfree/2020/aug/03/with-borders-closed-our-lifelines-to-family-overseas-have-been-cut-the-isolation-is-suffocating

Fenwick, George (2021), 'Kiwi stuck in UK wants to reconnect: "I'm becoming a stranger to the people I love"', *Stuff*, https://www.stuff.co.nz/life-style/life/300438512/kiwi-stuck-in-uk-wants-to-reconnect-im-becoming-a-stranger-to-the-people-i-love

FIGT (2022), 'FIGT Conference 2022', https://www.figt.org/conference2022

MacRae, Graeme (1 Jan 2020), Email to ASAANZ (Association of Social Anthropologists of Aotearoa/New Zealand).

Settles, Barbara H. (2001), 'Being at Home in a Global Society: A Model for Families' Mobility and Immigration Decisions', *Journal of Comparative Family Studies*, Vol. 32, iss. 4, pp. 627-645

ABOUT THE AUTHOR

Helen Ellis is a New Zealand researcher, writer, anthropologist and a veteran of distance grandparenting. Three of her four children and five of her six grandchildren live 16 to 30 flight hours away in America, England and Scotland. She is the founder of DistanceFamilies.com.

In her research, she asks: "How is Distance Familying for you?" Helen feels passionately that all generations of Distance Families deserve a voice and has single-handedly and doggedly taken on that role. Her goal is to support each generation to understand how it is for the other.

"With understanding comes empathy, and this can only do good as we all gingerly navigate the often challenging social phenomenon of Distance Families," she explains.

This is the second of a three-book series about Distance Families - each publication focusing on a different generation (grandparents, sons and daughters, and grandchildren). Helen encourages *all* generations to read *all* three books.

For an update on all titles, please visit www.DistanceFamilies.com.

ACKNOWLEDGEMENTS

I wish to thank those who have partnered alongside me for this, my second book.

First, there are hundreds of Distance Sons and Daughters who have no idea what they have taught me. I needed to learn 'how it is' being an expat/migrant *before* I could write about 'how it is' being a Distance Son or Daughter. For years I have quietly followed your blogs, podcasts and social media posts and read your books. Thank you for sharing your vulnerable selves.

I thank all the Distance Son and Daughter experts who opened up their Zoom windows for chats, especially Cath Brew, who took on a writing task. Your shared wisdom and belief that this book needed to be written spurred me on.

I thank my beta/advance readers and reviewers for doing more than just reading my manuscript. They also shared their thoughts and ideas. My book is better for everyone's input.

And then there are the global professionals who make a book shine. I am grateful for Jo Parfitt's no-nonsense editorial advice and Paddy Hartnett's methodical while charming editing and proofreading services. Each of Cath Brew's sketches tells an emotional story that so many relate to, and her cover design continues to be a hit. Closer to home, David Brown at BookPrint Ltd has been a stalwart of support, publicist Karen McKenzie shared her passion for my topic and Andrew Tizzard from distributor Nationwide Books welcomed me on board again.

Clive, my husband, has never budged in his belief in this book series project. In this edition I'm blessed and proud to share a little of his wisdom from decades of caring for clients. Abroad and at home, my mother and our children and grandchildren remain staunch supporters, even when they continue to see their lives in print.

A writer's life is a solitary one. Although I sit at my desk in New Zealand, thousands of miles away from so many, I have never felt alone. Scattered around the world are followers, cheerleaders, and, I'm humbled to say, even fans. Your messages, posts and words of encouragement fuel my journey. Thank you.

Helen Ellis

Founder

www.DistanceFamilies.com

Auckland, New Zealand

REVIEWS

Dear Reader,

Thank you for reading *Being a Distance Son or Daughter*, the second in the Distance Families series.

If you enjoyed this book, please post a brief review on your favourite digital platform. This spreads the word and is incredibly helpful to an author.

You may scan the QR code above for quick access to platforms or visit www.distancefamilies.com/write-a-review.html.

Thank you.

Helen Ellis

SOCIAL MEDIA LINKS

Like to keep the conversation going?

I would love to hear from you.

Helen Ellis

Monthly Newsletter:
www.distancefamilies.com/news

LinkedIn:
www.linkedin.com/in/helen-ellis-02590a16

Instagram:
@helenellis.author

Facebook:
Distance Families www.facebook.com/DistanceFamilies

Being a Distance Grandparent (Private Group)
www.facebook.com/groups/distancegrandparent

#distancefamilies

#beingadistancegrandparent

#beingadistancesonordaughter

#beingadistancegrandchild

Also in the *Being a Distance* Series:

For an update on these titles please visit www.DistanceFamilies.com.

BEING A
Distance Grandchild
A BOOK FOR ALL GENERATIONS
HELEN ELLIS M.A.

www.ingramcontent.com/pod-product-compliance
Ingram Content Group UK Ltd.
Pitfield, Milton Keynes, MK11 3LW, UK
UKHW020425250726
13967UKWH00007B/2818

9 780473 623418